Send Me A Copy!

Send Me A Copy!

A compilation of some of the
best messages ever sent through
the workplace (2009-2012)

Compiled by
Robert D. Kramer

ISBN 13: 978-0-9895028-0-1

Published in the United States of America

Table of Contents

Introduction

As a background, I am a United States Air Force Vet and I have spent over 40-years employed in corporate America. Early on in my career, people would come up to me and give me a piece of paper with some sort of joke, story, or just an item of interest to read. Usually I got a laugh from it or a comment such as: "That's Kool," and "Make me a copy of that." Then after the onrush of the computers in our business atmosphere, I would get emails from friends and acquaintances of these same type of jokes, stories or items of interest. I would usually laugh, and I almost always printed a copy. Some were dirty in nature, some political, some serious, some short and some had some length to them—you get the picture. I'm sure you have received them too.

I kept most all those copies over the years, and in this book I want to share them with you. I obviously transcribed them onto my computer for the book, but I wrote them just as they were received; spelling, punctuation, language, etc. I think if I put all the copies in a pile, it would probably be 12" to 15" high.

As you read this book, you may see a passage that is duplicated. That means different people sent me that communication in different years. Kind of like, it "keeps on giving."

I suspect, as you read these jokes/passages from our past, you will probably say to yourself, "I remember that!" And with others, you might say, "That was Kool," or "I can relate to that." Either way, I hope you enjoy the book as much as I have enjoyed receiving these jokes, stories and passages over the years.

2009

WHY ATHLETES CAN'T HAVE REAL JOBS

New Orleans Saint RB George Rogers when asked about the upcoming season: "I want to rush for 1,000 or 1,500 yards, which ever comes first."

Torrin Polk, University of Houston receiver, on his coach, John Jenkins: "He treats us like men. He lets us wear earrings."

Football commentator and former player Joe Theismann, 1996: "Nobody in football should be called a genius. A genius is a guy like Norman Einstein."

Senior basketball player at the University of Pittsburg: "I'm going to graduate on time, no matter how long it takes."

Bill Peterson, a Florida State football coach: "You guys line up alphabetically by height." And, "You guys pair up in groups of three, then line up in a circle."

Stu Grimson, Chicago Blackhawks left wing, explaining why he keeps a color photo of himself above his locker: "That's so when I forget how to spell my name, I can still find my clothes."

Lou Duva, veteran boxing trainer, on the Spartan training regime of heavyweight Andrew Golota: "He's a guy who gets up at six o'clock in the morning regardless of what time it is."

Chicago Cubs outfielder Andre Dawson on being a role model: "I wan' all them kids to do what I do, to look up at me. I wan' all the kids to copulate me."

Chuck Nevitt, North Carolina State basketball player, explaining to Coach Jim Valvano when he appeared nervous at practice: "My sister's expecting a baby, and I don't know if I'm going to be an uncle or an aunt."

Shelby Metcalf, basketball coach at Texas A&M, is recounting what he told a player who received four F's and one D: "Son, looks to me like you're spending too much time on one subject."

DIVORCE BARBIE

One day a father gets out of work and on his way home remembers that it's his daughter's birthday and asks the sales person, "How much for one of those Barbies in the display window?"

The sales person answers, "We have: Work Out Barbie for $19.95, Shopping Barbie for $19.95, Ballerina Barbie for $19.95, Astronaut Barbie for $19.95, Skater Barbie for $19.95 and Divorce Barbie for $265.95."

The amazed father asks: "Why is the Divorce Barbie at $265.95 and the others only $19.95?"

The annoyed salesperson rolls her eyes, sighs and answers: "Sir … Divorce Barbie comes with Ken's boat, Ken's furniture, Ken's computer, one of Ken's friends, and a keychain made with Ken's brass balls.

GOLFING NUN

A nun walks into Mother Superior's office and plunks down into a chair. She lets out a sigh heavy with frustration.

What troubles you, Sister?" asked the Mother Superior. "I thought this was the day you spent with your family.

"It was,: sighed the Sister. "And I went to play golf with my brother. We try to play golf as often as we could before I devoted my life to Christ."

I seem to recall that," the Mother Superior agreed. "So I take it your day of recreation was not relaxing.

"Far from it," snorted the Sister. "In fact, I even took the Lord's name in vain today!"

"Goodness, Sister!" gasped the Mother Superior, astonished. "You must tell me all about it!"

Well we were on the fifth tee … and this hole is a monster, Mother – 540 yard Par 5, with a nasty dogleg. I hit the drive of my life. I creamed it. The sweetest swing I ever made. And it's flying straight and true, right along the line I wanted … and it hits this bird in mid-flight!"

"Oh my!" commiserated the Mother. "How unfortunate! But surely that didn't make you blaspheme, sister."
"No, that wasn't it," admitted Sister. "While I was still trying to fathom what just happened, this squirrel appears from nowhere grabs my ball and runs down the fairway!"

"Oh, that would have made me blaspheme!" sympathized the Mother.

"But I didn't, Mother!" sobbed the Sister. "And I was so proud of myself! And while I was pondering what happened, this hawk swoops out of the sky and grabs the squirrel and flies off, with my ball still clutched in his paws!"

"So that's when you cursed," said the Mother with a knowing smile.

"Nope, that wasn't it either," cried the Sister, anguished, "because as the hawk started to fly out of sight, the hawk dropped him right there on the green, and the ball popped out of his paws and rolled to about 5 feet from the hole."

Mother Superior sat back in her chair, folded her arms across her chest, fixed the Sister with a baleful stare. "You missed the fucking putt, didn't you?"

A HEART WARMING STORY
FOR YOU GRANDPARENTS

A five-year-old boy and his grandpa are sitting on the front porch together, when gramps pulls a beer out of his cooler. The little boy asks: "Can I have a beer Grandpa?" Grandpa replies: "Can your pecker touch your ass?" The little boy answered: "No Grandpa, It's just a little pecker." Gramps says: "Well then, you're not man enough to have a beer."

A little later Grandpa lights up a cigar. The little boy asks: "Can I have a cigar Grandpa?" Once again, Grandpa asks: "Can your pecker touch your ass?" Once again the little boy replies, "No it's too little." Gramps replies, "Then you're not man enough to have a cigar."

A little later the little boy comes out of the house with milk and some cookies. Grandpa asks, "Hey there young feller, can I have a cookie?" The boy asks, "Can your pecker touch your ass?" Gramps replies, "Hell yes, my pecker can touch my ass." The little boy replies, "Then go fuck yourself, Grandma made these foe me."

THE COMPLAINT

Luke AFB is west of Phoenix and is rapidly being surrounded by civilization that complains about the noise from the base and its planes, forgetting that it was there long before they were. A certain lieutenant colonel at Luke AFB deserves a big pat on the back. Apparently, an individual who lives somewhere near Luke wrote the local paper complaining about a group of F-16's that disturbed his/her day at the mall.

When that individual read the response from a Luke AFB officer, it must have stung quite a bit.

'Question of the day for Luke Air Force base:

Whom do we thank for the morning air show? Last Wednesday, at precisely 9:11 A.M., a tight formation of four F-16 jets made a low pass over Arrowhead Mall, continuing west over Bell Road at approximately 500 feet. Imagine our good fortune! Do the Tom Cruise-wannabes feel we need this wake-up call, or were they trying to impress the cashiers at Mervyns early bird special?

Any response would be appreciated.

THE RESPONSE

Regarding a wake-up call from Luke's jets' on June 15, at precisely 9:12 A.M., a perfectly timed four-ship fly by of F-16's from the 63rd Fighter Squadron at Luke Air Force base flew over a grave of Capt. Jeremy Freques. Capt. Fresques was an Air Force officer who was previously stationed at Luke Air Force Base and was killed in Iraq on May 30, Memorial Day.

At 9:00 A.M. on June 15, his family and friends gathered at Sunland Memorial Park in Sun City to mourn the loss of a husband, son and friend. Based on the letter writer's recount of the fly-by, and because of the jet noise, I'm sure you didn't hear the 21-gun salute, the playing of taps, or my words to the widow and parents of Capt. Fresques as I gave them their son's flag on behalf of the President of the United States and all those veterans and servicemen and women who understand the sacrifices they endured.

A four-ship fly by is a display of respect the Air Force gives to those who give their lives in defense of freedom. We are professional aviators and take our jobs seriously, and on June 15, what the letter writer witnessed was four officers lining up to pay their ultimate respects.

The letter writer asks, "Whom do we thank for the morning air show?" The 56th Fighter Wing will make the call for you, and forward your thanks to the widow and parents of Capt Fresques, and thank them for you, for it was in their honor that my pilots flew the most honorable formation of their lives.

Only 2 defining forces have ever offered to die for you … Jesus Christ and the American Soldier. One died for your soul, the other for your freedom.

—Lt. Col. Grant L. Rosensteel, Jr.

RED SKELTON'S RECIPE FOR
THE PERFECT MARRIAGE

I know there is actually no such thing like as the perfect marriage and the Easter Bunny, but use your imagination anyway. There is the late great old comedian Red Skelton's recipe for the perfect marriage!

1. Two times a week we go to a nice restaurant, have a little beverage, good food and companionship. She goes on Tuesdays; I go on Fridays.

2. We also sleep in separate beds. Hers in California and mine is in Texas.

3. I take my wife where she wanted to go for our anniversary. 'Somewhere I haven't been in a long time!' she said. So I suggested the kitchen.

4. I take my wife everywhere … but she keeps finding her way back.

5. We always hold hands. If I let go, she shops.

6. She has an electric blender, electric toaster and electric bread maker. She said, 'There are too many gadgets, and no place to sit down!' So I bought her an electric chair.

7. My wife told me the car wasn't running well because there was water in the carburetor. I asked where the car was. She told me, 'In the lake.'

8. She got a mudpack, and looked great for two days. Then the mud fell off.

9. She ran after the garbage truck, yelling, 'Am I too late for the garbage?' The driver said, 'No, jump in!'

10. Remember: Marriage is the number one cause of divorce.

11. I married to Ms. Right. I just didn't know her first name was Always.

12. I haven't spoke to my wife in 18 months. I don't like to interrupt her.

13. The last fight was my fault, though. My wife asked, 'What's on the TV?' I said, 'Dust.'

THE WEDDING ANNOUNCEMENT

You are Regretfully Invited
To the Wedding between my Perfect Son ...

The Doctor

And Some ...

Cheap Two–Bit Tramp

Whose Name Escapes Me Right Now

The Biggest Disaster in My Family's History Will Take Place At:

9 pm on Saturday, September 8th

And No Doubt End In Divorce.
Hopefully In Time To Still Be Eligible For An Annulment.
The Overwhelmingly Disappointing Heartbreak of a Ceremony Will Be Followed By Dinner, Where Nuts Will Be Served Because Whatherface Has An Allergy.

AFTER THE 2008 ELECTION

The election is over. It is time to repair friendships with the other party. Governor Sarah Palin is doing her part to do just that.

The rest of the world cannot understand how, after bitter election campaigns, American politicians can kiss and make-up/

For instance, Gov. Palin has invited, to her great state of Alaska, the men who defeated her, Barack Obama and Joe Biden. She has set up a moose hunting trip for their enjoyment and hired three prominent experts in their field to assist them.

Dick Cheney will lead them on the hunt, Ted Kennedy will drive them back to their cabins each evening, and Bill Clinton will entertain their wives and daughters while the hunters are in field.

What a lady! That Sarah is such a sport and thinks of everything!

BIG PEOPLE WORDS

A group of children were trying very hard to become accustomed to Nursery School. The biggest hurdle they faced was that the teacher insisted on NO baby talk!

You need to use 'Big People words', she was always reminding them. She asked John what he had done over the weekend.

"I went to visit my Nana'. No, you went to visit your GRANDMOTHER. 'Use Big People words!'

She then asked Mitchell what he had done. "I took a ride on a choo-choo'. She said, 'No, you took a ride on a TRAIN. You must remember to use Big People words'.

She then asked little Alex what he had done? 'I read a book' he replied. 'That's WONDERFUL!' the teacher said, "What book did you read?" Alex thought real hard about it, then puffed out his chest with great pride, and said, 'Winnie the SHIT'.

THE POWER OF BILLY GRAHAM

Billy Graham was returning to Charlotte after a speaking engagement and when his Plane arrived there his limo was prepared to take him home. As he prepared to get into the limo, he stopped and spoke to the driver.

'You know' he said, 'I am 87 years old and I have never driven a limousine. Would you mind if I drove it for a while?' The driver said, 'No problem. Have at it.'

Billy gets into the driver's seat and they head off down the highway. A short distance away sat a rookie State Trooper operating his first speed trap.

The long black limo went by him doing 70 in a 55 mph zone. The young trooper pulled out and easily caught the limo and he got out of his patrol car to begin the procedure. The young trooper walked up to the driver's door and when the glass was rolled down, he was surprised to see who was driving.

He immediately excused himself and went back to his car and called his supervisor. He told the supervisor, 'I know we are supposed to enforce the law … but I also know that important people are given certain courtesies. I need to know what I should do because I have stopped a very important person.'

The supervisor asked, 'Is it the governor?' The young trooper said 'No, he's more important than that.'

The supervisor said, 'Oh, so it's the president.' The young trooper said, 'No, he's even more important than that.'

The supervisor finally asked, 'Well then, who is it?' The young trooper said, 'I think it's Jesus, because he's got Billy Graham for a chauffeur.'

DADDY'S LITTLE GIRL

A father watched his young daughter playing in the garden. He smiled as he reflected on how sweet and pure his little girl was. Tears formed in his eyes as he thought about her seeing the wonder of such innocent eyes.

Suddenly she just stopped and stared at the ground. He went over to her to see what work of God had captured her attention. He noticed she was looking at two spiders mating.

'Daddy, what are those two spiders doing?' she asked. 'They're mating,' her father replied.

'What do you call the spider on top?' she asked. That's a Daddy Longlegs.' Her father answered.

'So the other one is a Mommy Longlegs?' the little girl asked. As his heart soared with the joy of such a cute and innocent question, he said, 'Both of them are Daddy Longlegs.'

'The little girl, looked a little puzzled, thought for a moment, and then she stomped them flat. 'Well, we're not having any of that gay shit in our garden,' she said.

WHAT'S IN A NAME?

A woman scanned the guest at a party and spotted an attractive man standing alone.

She approached him. "My name is Carmen," she told him. "That's a beautiful name," he replied, "Is it a family name?"

"No," she replied. "I gave it to myself. It reflects the things I like most … cars and men."

"What's your name?" she asked. He said, "B.J. Titsengolf."

THE DIFFERENCE BETWEEN
GRANDMOTHERS AND GRANDFATHERS

A friend, who worked away from home all week, always made a special effort with his family on the weekends. Every Sunday morning he would take his 7-year old granddaughter out for a drive in the car for some bonding time. Just he and his granddaughter.

One particular Sunday however, he had a bad cold and really didn't feel like being up at all. Luckily, his wife came to the rescue and said that she would take their granddaughter out.

When they returned, the little girl anxiously ran upstairs to see her grandfather. 'Well, did you enjoy your ride with grandma?' 'Oh, yes, Papa' the girl replied, and do you know what? We didn't see a single dumb bastard or lousy shit head anywhere we went today.'

Brings a tear to your eye doesn't it?

BRAIN TRANSPLANT

In the hospital the relatives gathered in the waiting room, where a family member lay gravely ill. Finally, the doctor came in looking tired and somber.

'I'm afraid I'm the bearer of bad news.' He said as he surveyed the worried faces. 'The only hope left for your loved one at this time is a brain transplant. It's an experimental procedure, very risky, but it is the only hope. Insurance will cover the procedure, but you will have to pay for the BRAIN.'

The family members sat silent as they absorbed the news. After a time, someone asked, 'How much will the brain cost?' The doctor quickly responded, '$5,000 for a male brain and $200 for a female brain.'

The moment turned awkward. Some of the men actually had to try not to smile, avoiding eye contact with the women. A man unable to control his curiosity, finally blurter out the question everyone wanted to ask. 'Why is the male brain so much more than a female brain?'

The doctor smiled at the childish innocence and explained to the entire group. 'It's just standard pricing procedure. We have to price the female brains a lot lower because they've been used.'

THE MIND OF A SIX YEAR OLD

A teacher was reading the story of the Three Little Pigs to her class. She came to the part of the story where the first pig was trying to gather the building materials for his home. She read, 'and so the pig went up to the man with the wheelbarrow full of straw and said; 'Pardon me sir, but may I have some of that straw to build my house?'

The teacher paused then asked the class: 'And what do you think the man said?'

One little boy raised his hand and said very matter-of-factly … 'I think the man would have said – 'Well, I'll be damned!! A talking pig!'

HOW TO DRIVE IN JERSEY

Seriously, there are only two things needed to drive effectively in NJ: A horn and a middle finger. Everything else is superfluous, including knowing where you are going.

For those of you who live in Jersey or have lived there, these things may come as no surprise. For those who haven't traveled there before, beware, be prepared and be afraid … be very afraid.

1. You must first learn to pronounce the city name, it is Nork – rhymes with Fork, now New-ard. Also, Trenton is not pronounced Tren-ton, it is Trent-in.

2. The morning rush hour is from 5 AM to noon. The evening rush hour is from noon to 7 PM. Friday's rush hour starts on Thursday morning.

3. The minimum acceptable speed on the turnpike is 85 mph. On the parkway it's 105 or 110. Anything less is considered "Sissy."

4. Forget the traffic rules you learned elsewhere. Jersey has its own version of traffic rules. For example, cars/trucks with the loudest muffler go first at a four-way stop; the trucks with the biggest tires go second; However, in Monmouth and Burlington counties, SUV-driving, cell phone-talking moms ALWAYS have the right of way.

5. If you actually stop at a yellow light, you will be rear-ended, cussed out, and possibly shot.

6. Never honk at anyone. Ever! Seriously. It's another offense that can get you shot.

7. Road construction is permanent and continuous in all of Jersey. Detour barrels are moved around for your

entertainment pleasure during the middle of the night to make the next day's driving a bit more exciting.

8. Watch carefully for road hazards such as drunks, skunks, dogs, cats, barrels, cones, celebs, rubber-neckers, shredded tires, cell- phones, deer and other road kill, and the Homeless feeding on any of these items.

9. Map Quest does NOT work here – none of the roads are where they say they are or go where they say they do and all the Turnpike EZ Pass lanes are moved each night once again to make your ride more exciting.

10. If someone actually has their Turn Single ON, wave them to the shoulder immediately to let them know it has been "accidentally activated."

11. If you are in the left lane and only driving 70 in a 55-65 mph zone, you are considered a road hazard and will be "flipped off" accordingly. If you return the flip, you'll be shot.

12. Do not try to estimate travel time – just leave Monday afternoon for Tuesday appointments, by noon Thursday for Friday appointments, and right after church on Sunday for anything on Monday morning.

Drive Safely!

THE MOST FUNCTIONAL ENGLISH WORD

Well, it's shit … that's right. It's true, shit.

You can smoke shit, buy shit, sell shit, lose shit, forget shit, and tell others to eat shit. Some people know their shit, while others can't tell the difference between shit and shineola.

There are lucky shits, dumb shits, and crazy shits. There is bull shit, horse shit, and chicken shit. You can throw shit, sling shit, catch shit, shoot the shit, or duck when the shit hits the fan.

You can give a shit or serve shit on a shingle. You can find yourself in deep shit or be happier than a pig in shit.

Some days are colder than shit, some day are hotter than shit, and some days are just plain shitty. Some music sounds like shit, things can look like shit, and there are times when you feel like shit. You can have too much shit, not enough shit, the right shit, the wrong shit or a lot of weird shit.

You can carry shit, have a mountain of shit, or find yourself up shit creek without a paddle. Sometimes everything you touch turns to shit and other times you fall in a bucket of shit and come out smelling like a rose. When you stop to consider all the facts, it's the basic building block of the English language.

And remember, once you know your shit, you don't need to know anything else! Well, shit, it's time for me to go. Just wanted you to know that I do give a shit and hope you had a nice day without a bunch of shit, but if you happened to catch a load of shit from some shit-head ….. Well, Shit Happens!!!

LAST REQUEST

Katie Couric, Charlie Gibson, Brian Williams and a tough old U.S. Marine Sergeant were captured by terrorist in Iraq. The leader of the terrorists told them he'd grant each of them one last request before they were beheaded and dragged naked through the streets.

Katie Couric said, "Well, I'm a southerner, so I'd like one last plate of fried chicken." The leader nodded to an underling who left and returned with the chicken. Couric ate it all and said, "Now I can die content."
Charlie Gibson said, "I'm living in New York, so I'd like to hear the song, The Moon and Me, one last time." The terrorist leader nodded to another terrorist who had studied the Western world and knew the music. He returned with some rag-tag musicians and played the song. Gibson was satisfied.

Brian Williams said, "I'm a reporter to the end, I want to take out my tape recorder and describe the scene here and what's about to happen. Maybe, someday, someone will hear it and know that I was on the job till the end." The leader directed an aide to hand over the tape recorder and Williams dictated his comments. He then said, "Now I can die happy."

The leader turned and asked "And now, Mr. U.S. Marine, what is your final wish?" "Kick me in the ass," said the marine. "What?" asked the leader, "Will you mock us in your last hour?"

"No, I'm not kidding, I want you to kick me in the ass," insisted the Marine. So the leader shoved him into the yard and kicked him in the ass.

The marine went sprawling, but rolled to his knees, pulled a 9 mm pistol from inside his cammies and shot the leader dead. In the resulting confusion, he emptied his sidearm on six terrorists, then with his knife he slashed the throat of one, and with an AK-47, which he took, sprayed the rest of the terrorists killing another 11. In a flash, all of them were either dead or fleeing fro their lives.

As the Marine was untying Couric, Gibson and Williams, they asked him. "Why didn't you just shoot them all in the first place? Why did you ask him to kick you in the ass?"

"What?" replied the Marine, "and have you three assholes report that I was the aggressor…?"

Semper Fi!

CATHOLIC GOLF

A Catholic priest and a nun were taking a rare afternoon off and enjoying a round of golf. The priest stepped up to the first tee and took a mighty swing. He missed the ball entirely and said "shit, I missed."

The good Sister told him to watch his language. On his next swing, he missed again "Shit, I missed." "Father, I'm not going to play with you if you keep swearing," the nun said tartly. The priest promised to do better and the round continued.

On the 4th tee, he missed again. The usual comment followed. Sister is really mad now and says, "Father John, God is going to strike you dead if you keep swearing like that."

On the next tee, Father John swings and misses again. "Shit I missed." A terrible rumble is hears and a gigantic bolt of lightning comes out of the sky and strikes Sister Marie dead in her tracks.

And from the sky comes a booming voice … "Shit, I missed."

THE CANDY WITH THE LIL HOLE

In a first grade classroom, the children began to identify the flavors by their color in a LifeSavers roll.

Red …………… Cherry
Yellow ……….. Lemon
Green ………… Lime
Orange ……….. Orange

Finally the teacher gave them all Honey lifesavers. None of the children could identify the taste.

The teacher said, 'I will give you a clue. It's what your mother may sometimes call your father.'

One little girl looked up in horror, spit her lifesaver out and yelled, 'Oh my God! They're ass-holes!" The teacher left the room.

CRAIG'S LIST

Posted to Craig's List / Personals: "To the guy who tried to mug me in downtown Savannah night before last."

Date: 2009-05-27. 1:43 AM EST. I was the guy wearing the black Burberry jacket that you demanded that I hand over, shortly after you pulled the knife on me and my girlfriend threatening our lives. You also asked for my girlfriend's purse and earrings. I can only hope that you somehow come across this rather important message.

First, I'd like to apologize for your embarrassment; I didn't expect you to actually crap in your pants when I drew my pistol after you took my jacket. The evening was not that cold, and I was wearing the jacket for a reason. My girlfriend had just bought me that Kimber Model 1911 .45 A CP pistol for my birthday, and we had picked up a shoulder holster for it that very evening. Obviously you agree that it is a very intimidating weapon when pointed at your head … isn't it! I know it probably wasn't fun walking back to wherever you'd come from with that brown sludge in your pants. I'm sure it was even worse walking bare footed since I made you leave your shoes, cell phone, and wallet with me. (That prevented you from calling or running to your buddies to come help mug us again).

After I called your mother, or 'Momma' as you had her listed in your cell, I explained the entire episode of what you'd done. Then I went and filled up my gas tank as well as four other people in the gas station on your credit card. The guy with the big motor home took 150 gallons and was extremely grateful! I gave your shoes to a homeless guy outside Vinnie Van Go Go's, along with all the cash in your wallet. (That made his day!) I then threw your wallet into the big pink "pimp mobile" that was parked at the curb ... after I broke the windshield and side window and keyed the entire driver's side of the car.

Later, I called a bunch of phone sex numbers from your cell phone. Ma Bell just now shut down the line, although I only used the phone for a little over a day now, so what's going on with that? Earlier, I managed to get in two threatening phone calls to the DA's office and one to the FBI, while mentioning President Obama as my possible target. The FBI guy seemed really intense and we had a nice long chat (I guess while he traced your number etc.) In a way, perhaps I should apologize for not killing you ... but I feel this type of retribution is for a far more appropriate punishment for your threatened crime. I wish you well as you try to sort through some of these rather immediate pressing issues, and can only hope that you have the opportunity to reflect upon, and perhaps reconsider the career path you've chosen to pursue in life. Remember, the next time you might not be so lucky. Have a good day!

Thoughtfully yours,
Alex

P.S. – Remember this motto ... An Armed society makes for a more civil society!

REDNECK GIFTING

"Hello, is this the Sheriff's Office?"

"Yes. What can I do for you?"

"I'm calling to report 'bout my neighbor Floyd … He's a hidden' marijuana inside his firewood! Don't quite know how he gets it inside them logs, but he's hidden' it there."

"Thank you very much for the call, sir."

The next day, the Sheriff Deputies descend on Floyd's house. They search the shed where the firewood is kept. Using axes, they bust open every piece of wood, but find no marijuana. They sneer at Floyd and leave.

Shortly, the phone rings at Floyd's house. "Hey, Floyd! This here's Tom … Did the Sheriff come?" "Yeah!" "Did they chop your firewood?" "Yep!"

Happy Birthday, buddy!"

WHAT'S A GIRL TO DO?

A woman was in town on a shopping trip. She began her day finding the most perfect shoes in the first shop and a beautiful dress on sale in the second.

In the third, everything had just been reduced by 50% when her cell phone rang. It was a female doctor notifying her that her husband had just been in a terrible car accident and was in critical condition and in the ICU. The woman told the doctor to inform her husband where she was and that she'd be there as soon as possible.

As she hung up she realized she was leaving what was shaping up to be her best day ever in the boutiques. She decided to get in a couple more shops before heading to the hospital.

She ended up shopping the rest of the morning, finishing her trip with a cup of coffee and a beautiful chocolate cake slice, compliments of the last shop. She was jubilant.

Then she remembered her husband. Feeling guilty, she dashed to the hospital. She saw the doctor in the corridor and asked about her husband's condition. The female doctor glared at her and shouted, "You went ahead and finished your shopping trip didn't you? I hope you're proud of yourself! While you were out for the past four hours enjoying yourself in town, your husband has been languishing in the Intensive Care Unit! It's just as well you went ahead and finished, because it will more than likely be the last shopping trip you ever take! For the rest of his life he will require round-the-clock care. And he will now be your career!"

The woman was feeling so guilty she broke down and sobbed. The lady doctor then chuckled and said, "I'm just pulling your leg. He's dead. Show me what you bought."

KITCHEN WISDOM BETWEEN
MATTHA STEWART AND MAXINE

M.S.: Stuff a miniature marshmallow in the bottom of an ice cream cone to prevent ice cream drips.
Max: Just suck the ice cream out of the bottom of the cone, for Pete's sake! You are probably lying on the couch with your feet up eating it anyway!

M.S.: To keep potatoes from budding, place an apple in the bag with the potatoes.
Max: Buy Hungry Jack mashed potato mix. Keeps in the pantry for up to a year.

M.S.: When a cake recipe calls for flouring the baking pan, use a bit of the dry cake mix instead and there won't be any white mess on the outside of the cake.
Max: Go to the bakery! Hell, they'll even decorate it for you!

M.S.: If you accidentally over-salt a dish while it's still cooking, drop in a peeled potato and it will absorb the excess salt for an instant 'fix-me-up.'
Max: If you over-salt a dish while you are cooking, that's too bad. Please recite with me the real woman's motto: 'I made it, you will eat it and I don't care how bad it tastes!'

M.S.: Wrap celery in aluminum foil when putting in the refrigerator and it will keep for weeks.
Max: Celery? Never heard of it!

M.S.: Brush some beaten egg white over pie crust before baking to yield a beautiful glossy finish.

Max: The Mrs. Smith frozen pie directions do no include brushing egg whites over the crust, so I don't.

M.S.: Cure for headaches: take a lime, cut it in half and rub it on your forehead. The throbbing will go away.
Max: Take the lime, mix it with tequila, chill and drink! All your pains go away!

M.S.: If you have a problem opening jars, try using latex dish washing gloves. They give a non-slip grip that makes opening jars easy.
Max: Go ask that every cute neighbor if he can open it for you.

M.S.: Don't throw out all that leftover wine. Freeze into ice cubes for future use in casseroles and sauces
Max: Leftover wine????????????????????? HELLO!!!!!!!!!!!!!!

GETTING OLDER

To make it stand, you wet it!
To make it wet, you suck it!
To make it stiff, you lick it!
To get in, your push it!

Damn! Threading a needle when you're older is a BITCH.

HOW TO CALL THE POLICE WHEN YOU'RE OLD AND DON'T MOVE FAST ANYMORE

George Phillips, an elderly man, from Meridian, Mississippi, was going up to bed, when his wife told him that he'd left the light on in the garden shed, which she could see from the bedroom window. George opened the back door to go turn off the light, but saw that there were people in the shed stealing things.

He phoned the police, who asked, "Is someone in your house?"

He said "No, but some people are breaking into my garden shed and stealing from me" Then the police dispatcher said, "All patrols are busy. You should lock your doors and an officer will be along when one is available."

George said, "Okay." He hung up the phone and counted to 30. Then he phoned the police again.

"Hello, I just called you a few seconds ago because there were people stealing things from my shed. Well, you don't have to worry about them now because I just shot them," and he hung up.

Within five minutes, six Police Cars, a SWAT Team, a Helicopter, two Fire Trucks, a Paramedic, and an Ambulance showed up at the Phillips' residence, and caught the burglars red-handed.

One of the Policemen said to George, "I thought you said that you'd shot them!" George said, "I thought you said there was nobody available!"

Moral to the story – don't mess with old people.

TOWEL HEADS

Recently I received a warning about the use of this politically incorrect term, so please note: We all need to be more sensitive in our choice of words. I have been informed that the Islamic terrorists, who hate our guts and want to kill us, do not like to be called, "Towel Heads," since the item they wear on their heads is not actually a towel, but in fact, a small folded sheet. Therefore, from this point forward, please refer to them as "Little Sheet Heads". Thank you for your support and compliance on this delicate matter.

THE THREE LITTLE PIGS – ITALIAN STYLE

Once upon a time there were three little pigs. The straw pig, the stick pig and the brick pig.

One day this nasty old wolf came up to the straw pig's house and said, "I'm going to huff and puff and blow your house down." And he did!!

So the straw pig went running over to the stick pig's house and said, "Please let me in, the wolf just blew down my house." So the stick pig let the straw pig in.

Just then the wolf showed up and said, "I'm going to huff and puff and blow your house down." And he did!!

So the straw pig and the stick pig went running over to the brick pig's house and said, "Let us in, let us in, the big bad wolf just blew our houses down!"

So the brick pig let them in just as the wolf showed up. The wolf said, "I'm going to huff and puff and blow your house down." The straw pig and the stick pig were so scared! But the brick pig picked up the phone and made a call.

A few minutes passed and a big, black Caddy pulls up.

Out step two massive pigs in pin striped suits and fedora hats. These pigs come over to the wolf, grab him by the neck and beat the living shit out of him, then one of them pulled out a gun, stuck it in his mouth and fired, killing the wolf, then they tied cement blocks around his feet, threw his sorry ass into the creek, then they got back into their Caddy and drove off.

The straw pig and stick pig were amazed!! "Who the hell were those guys?" they asked. "Those were my cousins … the Guinea Pigs.

THE PATCH

The other day I needed to go to the emergency room. Not wanting to sit there for 4 hours, I put on my old Army fatigues and stuck a patch onto the front of my shirt that I had downloaded off the Internet.

When I went into the E.R., I noticed ¾ of the people got up and left. I guess they decided that they weren't that sick after all. Cut at least 3 hours off my waiting time.

The parch read "U.S. Border Patrol".

It also works well at DMV. It saved me 5 hours. At the Laundromat, three minutes after entering, I had my choice of any machines most still running. Don't try it at McDonald's though … The whole crew got up and left and I never got my order.

JESUS IS WATCHING YOU

A burglar broke into a house one night. He shined his flashlight around, looking for valuables when a voice in the dark said, "Jesus knows you're here."

He nearly jumped out of his skin, clicked his flashlight off, and froze. When he heard nothing more, after a bit, he shook his head and continued.

Just as he pulled the stereo out so he could disconnect the wired, clear as a bell he heard, "Jesus is watching you."

Freaked out, he shined his light around frantically, looking for the source of the voice. Finally, in the corner of the room, his flashlight beam came to rest on a parrot.

"Did you say that." He hissed at the parrot. "Yep", the parrot confessed, then squawked, "I'm just trying to warn you that he is watching you."

The burglar relaxed. "Warn me, huh? Who in the world are you?"

"Moses," replied the bird. "Moses?" the burglar laughed. "What kind of people would name a bird Moses?"

"The same kind of people that would name a Rottweiler Jesus."

CALMNESS IN OUR LIVES

I am passing this on to you because it definitely works and we could all use a little more calmness in our lives. By following a simple advice heard on the Oprah show, you too can find inner peace.

Dr. OZ proclaimed, "The way to achieve inner peace is to finish all the things you have started and have never finished."

I looked around the house to see all the things I started and hadn't finished, and before leaving the house this morning. I finished off a bottle of Zinfandel, a bottle of Tequila, a package of Oreos, the remainder of my old Prozac prescription, the rest of the cheesecake, some Doritos, and a box of chocolates.

You have no idea how freaking good I feel right now!

SENIOR HEALTH CARE SOLUTION

So you're a senior citizen and the government says no health care for you, what do you do?

Our plan gives anyone 65 years or older a gun with 4 bullets. You are allowed to shoot 2 Senators and 2 Representatives. Of course, this means you will be sent to prison.
There you will get 3 meals a day, a roof over your head, and all the health care you need! New teeth, no problem. Need glasses, great. New hip, knees, kidney, lungs, heart? All covered.

And who will be paying for all of this? The same government that just told you that you are too old for health care. Plus, because you are a prisoner, you don't have to pay any income taxes anymore.

YOU COULD HAVE HEARD A PIN DROP

At a time when our president and other politicians tend to apologize for our countries prior to actions, here's a refresher on how some of your former patriots handled negative comments about our country.

1. Secretary of State, Dean Rusk, was in France in the early 60's when DeGaule decided to pull out of NATO. DeGaule said he wanted all US military out of France as soon as possible.

Rusk responded "does that include those who are buried here

2. When in England, at a fairly large conference, Colin Powell was asked by the Archbishop of Canterbury if our plans for Iraq were just an example of empire building by George Bush.

He answered by saying, "Over the years, the United States has sent many of its fine young men and women into great peril to fight for freedom beyond our borders. The only amount of land we have ever asked for in return is enough to bury those that did not return."

3. There was a conference in France where a number of international engineers were taking part, including French and American. During a break, one of the French engineers came back into the room saying "Have you heard the latest dumb stunt Bush has done" He has sent an aircraft carrier to Indonesia to help the tsunami victims. What does he intend to do, bomb them?"

Boeing engineer stood up and replied quietly: "Our carriers have three hospitals on board that can treat several hundred people; they are nuclear powered and can supply emergency electrical power to shore facilities; they have three cafeterias with the capacity to feed

3,000 people three meals a day, they can produce several hundred thousand gallons of fresh water from sea water each day, and they carry half a dozen helicopters for use in transporting victims and injured to and from their flight deck. We have eleven such ships; how many does France have?"

4. A U.S. Navy Admiral was attending a naval conference that included Admirals from the U.S., English, Canadian, Australian and French Navies. At a cocktail reception, he found himself standing with a large group of Officers that included personnel from most of those countries. Everyone was chatting away in English as they sipped their drinks, but the French Admiral suddenly complained that, whereas Europeans learn many languages, Americans learn only English. He then asked, "Why is it that we always have to speak English in these conferences rather than speaking French?"

Without hesitating, the American Admiral replied, "Maybe it's because the Brit's, Canadians, Aussie's and Americans arranged it so you wouldn't have to speak German."

5. Robert Whiting, an elderly gentleman of 83, arrived in Paris by plane. At French Customs, he took a few minutes to locate his passport in his carry on.

"You have been to France before, monsieur?" the customs officer asked sarcastically.

Mr. Whiting admitted that he had been to France previously.

"Then you should know enough to have your passport ready."

The American said, "The last time I was here, I didn't have to show it."

"Impossible. Americans always have to show your passport on arrival in France!"

The American senior gave the Frenchman a long hard look. Then quietly explained, "Well, when I came ashore at Omaha Beach on D-Day in 1944 to help liberate this country, I couldn't find a single Frenchman to show a passport to."

WHY NORTHERNERS BECOME SHOW BIRDS

December 8: 5PM – and it's beginning to snow, it's the first snowfall of the season and the wife and I took our hot rums and sat by the window. The soft snowflakes drifted down and it was an absolutely magnificent sight.

December 9: We woke this morning to a big wonderful blanket of crystal white snow covering the landscape. What a fantastic sight! Every tree and shrub covered with a pristine white mantle. I shoveled for the first time in years and it really felt good. I did the driveway and the sidewalk. Later, the snowplow came along and covered up the driveway with compact snow from the street. He smiled and waved – I waved back and smiled at him and I shoveled the driveway again.

December 12: The sun has melted most of our lovely snow. Oh well, I'm sure we will get a little more before winter is over.

December 14: It snowed 8 inches last night and the temperature has dropped to zero. I shoveled the sidewalk and driveway again. After I finished, the snowplow came along and did his trick.

December 15: Sold my car today and bought a 4X4 so we could get around in the snow easier. Also bought snow tires, just to be safe.

December 18: Fell on my ass on the ice in the driveway. Chiropractor charged me $25, but nothing was broken, thank God. The sky is getting dark again.

December 19: Still cold (minus 10 this morning) and the roads are icy, making driving difficult. I slid into the guardrail with my wife's car. Did $500 damage. She is all pissed off and gave me shit.

December 20: We had another 14 inches of the white shit again last night. More shoveling in store for me today. Damn snowplow by twice today!

December 22: We are assured of a White Christmas, because another 7 inches of the shit fell today and with the freezing weather it probably won't melt until next August. I got all dressed up to go out and shovel that shit again. Put on winter boots, jump suit, jacket, scarf, earmuffs, gloves, etc. and then got the urge to go piss, by now I need a bowel movement too.

December 24: If I ever catch the son-of-a-bitch that drives that snowplow, I'll drag him through the snow by his balls. I think he hides around the corner until I've finished shoveling, then he comes down the street at 100 miles per hour throwing that white shit everywhere he can.

December 25: MERRY CHRISTMAS!! … they predict 12 more inches of the fucking white shit again tonight. Does anyone know how many shovels full of snow 12 inches makes? To hell with Santa, he doesn't have to shovel all this white shit, just so HE can have a MERRY CHRISTMAS! That damn snowplow operator just came by asking for a donation to their Christmas Fund. I hit him with my fucking snow shovel. Doctors say he'll live – and I'm on 2 years probation

December 28: Don't eat the brown snow around our house because the toilet froze up and we have to piss outside. The roof is starting to cave-in and the well went dry.

December 30: I torched the damn house today, and we headed south.

January 4: We arrived in Florida today and some local asshole heading North with skis just gave me the finger. I hope the prick has to shovel his way out of Alberta snow storm in his bare ass at 40 below zero, until his balls drop off!!!

Signed - A Contented Snowbird.

YOU HAVE GOT TO LOVE MAXINE

If you woke up breathing, congratulations! You have another chance.

The only two things we do with greater frequency is middle age are urinate and attend funerals.

The trouble with bucket seats is that not everybody has the same size bucket.

To err is human, to forgive – highly unlikely.

Do you realize that in about 40 years, we'll have millions of old ladies running around with tattoos and pierced navels? (Now that's scary!)

Money can't buy happiness - - but somehow it's more comfortable to cry in a Porsche than a Kia.

After a certain age, if you don't wake up aching somewhere…you may be dead.

THE POPE AND PELOSI

The Pope and Nancy Pelosi are on the same stage in Yankee Stadium in front of a huge crowd.

The Pope leans towards Mrs. Pelosi and said, "Do you know that with one little wave of my hand I can make every person in this crowd go wild with joy? This joy will not be a momentary display, but will go deep into their hearts and they'll forever speak of this day and rejoice!"

Pelosi replied, "I seriously doubt that. With one little wave of your hand? Show me!"

So the Pope backhanded the bitch.

2010

GOD BLESS THE TEACHERS

After being interviewed by the school administration, the prospective teacher said:

"Let me see if I've got this right. You want me to go into that room with all those kids, correct their disruptive behavior, observe them for signs of abuse, monitor their dress habits, censor their T-shirt messages, and instill in them a love for learning.

You want me to check their backpacks for weapons, wage war on drugs and sexually transmitted diseases, and raise their sense of self esteem and personal pride. You want me to teach them patriotism and good citizenship, sportsmanship and fair play, and how to register to vote, balance a checkbook, and apply for a job.

You want me to check their heads for lice, recognize signs of antisocial behavior, and make sure that they all pass the final exams.

You also want me to provide them with an equal education regardless of their handicaps, and communicate regularly with their parents in English, Spanish or any other language, by letter, telephone, newsletter, and report card. You want me to do all this with a piece of chalk, a blackboard, a bulletin board, a few books, a big smile, and a starting salary that qualifies me for food stamps.

You want me to do all this and then to tell me … I can't PRAY!"

MEDICAL DISTINCTION BETWEEN
GUTS AND BALLS

There is a medical distinction between Guts and Balls. We've all heard about people having Guts or Balls, but do you really know the difference between them? In an effort to keep you informed, here are the definitions:

GUTS – Is arriving home late after a night out with the guys, being met by your wife with a broom, and having the guts to ask: "Are you still cleaning, or are you flying somewhere?

BALLS – Is coming home late after a night out with the guys, smelling of perfume and beer, lipstick on your collar, slapping your wife on the butt and having the Balls to say: "You're next, Chubby."

I hope this clears up any confusion on the definitions. Medically speaking, there is no difference in the outcome. Both result in death.

MY LIVING WILL

Last night, my kids and I were sitting in the living room and I said to them, "I never want to live in a vegetative state, dependent on some machine and fluids from a bottle. If that ever happens, just pull the plug."

They got up, unplugged the computer, and threw out my wine. They are such asses …

A LETTER HOME

Dear Ma and Pa:

I am well. Hope you are. Tell brother Walt and brother Elmer the Army beats working for old man Minch by a mile. Tell them to join up quick before all of the places are filled.

I was restless at first because you get to stay in bed till nearly 6 AM. But I am getting so I like to sleep late. Tell Walt and Elmer all you do before breakfast is smooth your cot, and shine some things.

No hogs to slop, feed to pitch, mash to mix, wood to split, fire to lay. Practically nothing. Men go to shave, but it is not so bad, there's warm water. Breakfast is strong on trimmings like fruit juice, cereal, eggs, bacon, etc., but weak on chops, potatoes, ham steak, fried eggplant, pie and other regular food, but tell Walt and Elmer you can always sit by the two city boys that live on coffee. Their food, plus yours, holds you until noon when you get fed again.

It's no wonder these city boys can't walk much. We go on 'routine marches,' which the platoon sergeant says are long walks to harden us. If he thinks so, it's not my place to tell him different. A 'routine march' is about as far as to our mailbox at home. Then the city guys get sore feet and we all ride back in trucks.

The sergeant is like a school teacher. He nags a lot. The Captain is like the school board. Majors and Colonel's just ride around and frown. They don't bother you none.

The next will kill Walt and Elmer with laughing. I keep getting medals for shooting. I don't know why. The bulls-eye is near as big as a chipmunk head and don't move, and it ain't shooting at you like the Higgett boys at home. All you got to do is lie there all comfortable and hit it. You don't even load your own cartridges. They come in boxes.

Then we have what they call hand-to-hand combat training. You get to wrestle with them city boys. I have to be real careful though, they break real easy. It ain't like fighting with that ole bull at home. I'm about the best they got in this except for that Tug Jordan from over in Silver Lake. I only beat him once. He joined up the same time as me, but I'm only 5'6" and 130 pounds, and he's 6'8" and near 300 pounds dry.

Be sure to tell Walt and Elmer to hurry and join before other fellers get onto this setup and come stampeding in.

Your loving daughter,

Alice

ENGLISH LESSON

Watch those prepositions!

On his 74th birthday, a man got a gift certificate from his wife. The certificate paid for a visit to a medicine man living on a nearby reservation that was rumored to have a wonderful cure for erectile dysfunction. After being persuaded, he drove to the reservation, handed his ticket to the medicine man and wondered what he was in for …

The old medicine man slowly, methodically produced a potion, handed it to him, and with a grip on his shoulder, warned, "This is powerful medicine and it must be respected. You take only a teaspoon and then say '1-2-3! When you do that, you will become more manly than you have ever been in your life and you can perform as long as you want."

The man was encouraged. As he walks away, he turned and asked, "How do I stop the medicine from working?"

The medicine man replied, "Your partner must say '1-2-3.' But when she does the medicine will not work again until the next full moon."

He was very eager to see if it worked so he went home, showered, shaved, took a spoonful of the medicine, and then invited his wife to join him in the bedroom. When she came in, he took off his clothes and said, "1-2-3!" Immediately, he was the manliest of men.

His wife became very excited and began throwing off her clothes. And then she asked, "What was the 1-2-3- for?"

And that, boys and girls, is why we should never end our sentences with a preposition because we could end up with a dangling participle.

PARKING TICKET

Working people frequently ask retired people what they do to make their days interesting.

Well, for example, the other day my wife and I went into town and went shop. We were only there for about 5 minutes. When we came out, there was a cop writing a parking ticket. We went up to him and said, "Come on man, how about giving a senior citizen a break. He ignored us and continued writing the ticket. I called him a Nazi turd. He glared at me and began writing another ticket for having worn tires.

So my wife called him a shit-heat. He finished the second ticket and put it on the windshield. Then he started writing a third ticket. This went on for about 20 minutes. The more we called him names, the more tickets he wrote.

Personally, we didn't care. We came into town by bus and the car had an Obama sticker on the bumper. We had so much fun. It's important at our age.

NEW WINE AT WAL-MART

Wal-Mart announced that, sometime in early 2010, it will begin offering customers a new discount item … Wal-Mart's own brand of wine. The world's largest retail chain is rumored to be teaming up with Ernest & Julio Gallo Winery of California to produce the spirits at an affordable price – in the $2 to $5 range.

Wine connoisseurs may not be inclined to put a bottle of the Wal-Mart brand into their shopping carts, but "There is a market for inexpensive wine," said Kathy Micken, professor of marketing at University of Arkansas, Bentonvillle. "However, branding will be very important."

Customer surveys were conducted to determine the most attractive name for the Wal-Mart wine brand. The top surveyed names in order of popularity were:

Chateau du Trailer Parc
White Trashfindel
Big Red Gulp
World Championship Riesling
NASCARbernet
Chef Boyardeaux
Peanut Noir
Ah Kain't Believe it's not Vinegar
Grape Expectations
Nasti Spumante

The beauty of Wal-Mart wine is that it can be served with either white meat (Possum) or red meat (Squirrel).

OLD GUY FROM MONTANA

The real shame is that you could address this letter to virtually all the Democrats and Republicans in the House and Senate.

You gotta watch these old guys from Montana… Uh…something tells me this guy might be a teensy bit pissed.

Senator Alan Simpson calls Seniors "Greediest Generation". Therefore this, from a man in Montana…who – like the rest of us – has just about had enough.

Hey Allan, let's get a few things straight…

1. As a career politician, you have been on the public dole for fifty years…

2. I have been paying Social Security taxes for 48 years (since I was 15 years old. I am now 63…)

3. My Social Security payments, and those of millions of other Americans, were safely tucked away in an interest bearing account for decades until you political pukes decided to raid the account and give OUR money to a bunch of zero ambition losers in return for votes, thus bankrupting the system and turning Social Security into a Ponzi scheme that would have made Bernie Madoff proud…

4. Recently, just like Lucy and Charlie Brown, you and your ilk pulled the proverbial football away from millions of Americans seniors nearing retirement and moved the goalposts for full retirement from age 65 to age 67. NOW, you and your shill commission is proposing to move the goalposts YET AGAIN…

5. I, and millions of other Americans, have been paying income taxes our entire lives, and now you propose to change the rules of the game. Why? Because you incompetent bastards spent our money so profligately that you just kept on spending even after you ran out of money. Now, you come to the American taxpayers and say you need more to pay off YOUR debt...

6. I, and millions of other Americans, have been paying into Medicare from Day One, and now you morons propose to change the rules of the game. Shy? Because you idiots mismanaged other parts of the economy to such an extent that you need to steal money from Medicare to pay the bills.

To add insult to injury, you label us "greedy" for calling "bullshit" on your incompetence. Well, Captain Bullshit, I have a few questions for YOU...

1. How much money have you earned from the American taxpayers during your pathetic 50-year political career?

2. At what age did you retire from your pathetic political career, and how much are you receiving in annual retirement benefits from the American taxpayers?

3. How much do you pay for YOUR government provided health insurance?

4. What cuts in YOUR retirement and healthcare benefits are you proposing in your disgusting deficit reduction proposal, or, as usual, have you exempted yourself and your political cronies?

It is you, Captain Bullshit, and your political co-conspirators who are "greedy". It is you and they who have bankrupted America and stolen the American dream from millions of loyal, patriotic taxpayers. And for what? Votes? That's right, sir. You and yours have bankrupted America for the sole purpose of advancing you pathetic political careers. You know it, we know it, and you know that we know it.

And you can take that to the bank!

LET ME SEE IF I GOT THIS RIGHT

- If you cross the North Korean Border illegally, you get 12 years hard labor.

- If you cross the Iranian Border illegally, you are detained indefinitely.

- If you cross the Afgan Border illegally, you get shot.

- If you cross the Saudi Arabian Border illegally, you will be jailed.

- If you cross the Chinese Border illegally, you may never be heard from again.

- If you cross the Venezuelan Border illegally, you will be branded a spy and your fate will be sealed.

- If you cross the Cuban Border illegally, you will be thrown into political prison to rot, BUT

- If you cross the U.S. Border illegally, you get

    - A job,
    - A drivers License,
    - Social Security Card,
    - Welfare,
    - Food Stamps,
    - Credit Cards,
    - Subsidized rent or a loan to buy a house,
    - Free education,
    - Free health care,
    - A lobbyist in Washington,

- Billions of dollars worth of public documents printed in your language,
- And the right to carry your country's flag while you protest that you don't have any rights.

I JUST WANTED TO MAKE SURE I HAD A FIRM GRASP OF THE SITUATION – BEFORE WE ELECT THE UNPRINCIPLED PIGS OUT OF CONGRESS IN NOVEMBER.

THE MIDDLE WIFE BY A 2ND GRADE TEACHER

I have been teaching now for about fifteen years. I have two kids myself, but the best birth story I know is the one I saw in my own second grade classroom a few years back.

When I was a kid, I loved show-and-tell. So I always have a few sessions with my students. It helps them get over shyness and usually, show-and-tell is pretty tame. Kids bring in per turtles, model airplanes, pictures of fish they catch, stuff like that. And I never, ever place any boundaries or limitations on them. If they want to lug it in to school and talk about it, they are welcome.

Well, one day this little girl, Erica, a very bright, very outgoing kid, takes her turn and waddles up to the front of the class with a pillow stuffed under her sweater. She holds up a snapshot of an infant. "This is Luke, my baby brother and I am going to tell you about his birthday."

"First, Mom and Dad made him as a symbol of their love and then Dad put a seed in my Mom's stomach and Luke grew in there. He ate for nine months through an umbrella cord."

She is standing there with her hands on the pillow and I am trying not to laugh and wishing I had a camcorder with me. The kids are watching her in amazement.

"Then, about two Saturdays ago, my Mom starts saying and going, 'Oh, Oh, Oh, Oh'!" Erica puts a hand behind her back and groans. "She walked around the house for, like an hour 'Oh, Oh, Oh'!" (Now this kid is doing a hysterical duck walk and groaning.)

"My Dad called the middle wife. She delivers babies, but she does not have a sign on the car like the Domino's man. They got my Mom to lie down in bed like this." (Then Erica lies down with her back against the wall.)

"And then, pop! My Mom had this bag of water she kept in there in case he got thirsty, and it just blew up and spilled all over the bed, like psshhheew!!" (This kid has her legs spread with her little hands miming water flowing away. It was too much!)

"Then the middle wife starts saying 'push, push, push, and breath, breathe'. They started counting but never even got past ten then all of a sudden, out comes my brother. He was covered in yucky stuff that they all said it was from Mom's play-center, (placenta) so there must be a lot of toys inside there. When he got out, the middle wife spanked him for crawling up in there."

The Erica stood up, took a big theatrical bow and returned to her seat. I am sure I applauded the loudest. Ever since then, when it is show-and-tell day, I bring my camcorder, just in case another 'Middle Wife' comes along.

THE DOT

Finally, someone has cleared this up.

For centuries, Hindu women have worn a dot on their foreheads.

Most of us have naively thought this was connected with tradition or religion, but the Indian embassy in Ottawa has recently revealed the true story.

When a Hindu woman gets married, she brings a dowry into the union. On her wedding night, the husband scratches off the dot to see whether he has won a convenience store, a gas station, a donut shop, a taxi cab, or a motel in Canada or the USA.

If nothing is there, he must remain in India to answer telephones and provide us with technical advice.

MY DOGS

This morning I went to sign my dogs up for welfare. At first the lady said, "Dogs are not eligible to draw welfare," So I explained to her that my dogs are mixed in color, unemployed, lazy, can't speak English and have no frigging clue who their Daddy's are. They expect me to feed them, provide them with housing and medical care. So she looked in her policy book to see what it takes to qualify. My dogs get their first checks Friday.

This is a great country!

THE GAY FLIGHT ATTENDANT

My flight was being served by an obviously gay flight attendant, who seemed to put everyone in a good mood as her served us food and drinks.

As the plane prepared to descend, he came swishing down the aisle and told us that "Captain Harvey has asked me to announce that he'll be landing the big scary plane shortly, so lovely people, if you could first put your trays up, that would be super."

On his trip back up the aisle, he noticed this well-dressed and rather Arabic looking woman hadn't moved a muscle. "Perhaps you didn't hear me over those big brute engines, but I asked you to raise your trazy-poo, so the main man can pitty-pat us on the ground".

She calmly turned her head and said, "In my country, I am called a Princess and I take orders from no one."

To which (I swear) the flight attendant replied, without missing a beat, "Well, sweet-cheeks, in my country I'm called a Queen, so I out rank you. Tray-up, Bitch!"

MUSLIM BELIEFS (THIS IS NOT A HATE WRITING)

This is a true story and the author, Rick Mathes, is a well-known leader in prison ministry.

The Muslim religion is the fastest growing religion per capita in the United States, especially within the minority races.

Last month I attended my annual training session that's required for maintaining my state prison security clearance. During the training session there was a presentation by three speakers representing the Roman Catholic, Protestant and Muslim faiths, who explained each of their beliefs.

I was particularly interested in what the Islamic Imam had to say. The Imam gave a great presentation of the basics of Islam, complete with a video. After the presentations, time was provided for questions and answers.

When it was my turn, I directed my question to the Imam and asked: "Please, correct me if I'm wrong, but I understand that most Imams and clerics of Islam have declared a holy jihad (Holy war) against the infidels of the world and, that by killing an infidel, (which is a command to all Muslims) they are assured of a place in heaven. If that's the case, can you give me the definition of an infidel?"

There was no disagreement with my statements and, without hesitation, he replied, "Non-believers!"

I responded, "So, let me make sure I have this straight. All followers of Allah have been commanded to kill everyone who is not of your faith so they can have a place in heaven. Is that correct?"

The expression on his face changed from one of authority and command to that of a little boy who had just been caught with his hand in the cookie jar. He sheepishly replied, "Yes".

I then stated, "Well, sir, I have a real problem trying to imagine Pope John Paul commanding all Catholics to kill those of your faith, or Dr. Stanley ordering all Protestants to do the same in order to guarantee them a place in heaven."

The Imam was speechless.

I continued, "I also have a problem with being your friend when you and your brother clerics are telling your followers to kill me? Let me ask you a question: Would you rather have your Allah, who tells you to kill me in order for you to go to heaven, or my Jesus who tells me to love you because I am going to heaven and He wants you to be there with me."

You could have heard a pin drop as the Imam hung his head (in shame?). Needless to say, the organizers and/or promoters of the Diversification training seminar were not happy with my way of dealing with the Islamic Imam, and exposing the truth about the Muslims' beliefs.

KULULA AIRLINES

Kalula is a low-cost South-African airline that doesn't take itself too seriously. Kulula airline attendants make an effort to make the in-flight safety lecture and announcements a bit more entertaining.

- "People, people we're not picking out furniture here, find a seat and get in it".

- On a flight with a very senior flight attendant crew, the pilot said, "Ladies and Gentlemen, we've reached cruising altitude and will be turning down the cabin lights. This is for comfort and to enhance the appearance of your flight attendants."

- On landing, the stewardess said, "Please be sure to take all of your belongings. If you're going to leave anything, please make sure it's something we'd like to have."

- "There may be 50 ways to leave your lover, but there are only 4 ways out of this airplane."

- "Thank you for flying Kulula. We hope you enjoyed giving us the business as much as we enjoyed taking you for a ride."

- As the plane landed and was coming to a stop at Durban Airport, a lone voice came over the loudspeaker: "Whoa, big fella. WHOA!"

- After a particularly rough landing during thunderstorms in the Karoo, a flight attendant announced, "Please take care when opening the overhead compartments because, after a landing like that, sure as hell everything has shifted."

- "Welcome aboard Kulula 271 to Port Elizabeth. To operate your seat belt, insert the metal tab into the buckle, and pull tight. It works just like every other seat belt; and, if you don't know how to operate one, you probably shouldn't be out in public unsupervised."

- "In the event of a sudden loss of cabin pressure, masks will descend from the ceiling. Stop screaming, grab the mask, and pull it over your face. If you have a small child traveling with you, secure your mask before assisting with theirs. If you are traveling with more than one small child, pick your favorites."

- "Weather at our destination is 50 degrees with some broken clouds, but we'll try to have them fixed before we arrive. Thank you, and remember, nobody love you, or your money, more than Kulula Airlines."

- "Your seat cushions can be used for flotation; and in the event of an emergency water landing, please paddle to shore and take them with our compliments."

- "As you exit the plane, make sure to gather all of your belongings. Anything left behind will be distributed evenly among the flight attendants. Please do not leave children or spouses."

- And from the pilot during his welcome message: "Kulula Airline is pleased to announce that we have some of the best flight attendants in the industry. Unfortunately, none of them are on this flight."

- After a hard landing the flight attendant said, "That was quite a bump and I know what y'all are thinking. I'm here to tell you it wasn't the airline's fault, it wasn't the pilot's fault, it wasn't the flight attendants fault, it was the asphalt."

- Overheard on a Kulula flight into Cape Town, on a particularly windy and bumpy day; during the final approach, the Captain really had to fight it. After an extremely hard landing, the Flight attendant said, "Ladies and Gentlemen, welcome to To Mother City. Please remain in your seats with your seat belts fastened while the Captain taxis what's left of our airplane to the gate."

- After another attendant's comment on a less than perfect landing: "We ask you to please remain seated as Captain Kangaroo bounces us to the terminal."

- An airline pilot wrote that on this particular flight he had hammered his ship into the runway really hard. The airline had a policy which required the first officer to stand at the door while the passengers exited, smile, and give them a "thanks for flying our airline." He said that, in light of his bad landing, he had a hard time looking the passengers in the eye, thinking that someone would have a smart comment. Finally everyone had gotten off except for a little old lady walking with a cane. She said, "Sir, do you mind if I ask you a question?" "Why, no Ma'am." Said the pilot. "What is it?" The little old lady said, "Did we land, or were we shot down?"

- After a real crusher of a landing in Johannesburg, the attendant came on with, "Ladies and Gentlemen, please remain in you seats until Captain Crash and the Crew have brought the aircraft to a screeching halt against the gate. And, once the tire smoke has cleared and the warning bells are silenced, we will open the door and you can pick your way through the wreckage to the terminal."

- "We'd like to thank you folks for flying with us today. And, the next time you get the insane urge to go blasting through the skies in a pressurized metal tube, we hope you'll think of Kulula Airlines."

- "Ladies and Gentlemen, if you wish to smoke, the smoking section on this airplane is on the wing. If you can light 'em, you can smoke 'em."

- "Ladies and Gentlemen, this is your captain speaking. Welcome to Flight Number 293, non-stop from Durban to Cape Town, the weather ahead is good and, therefore, we should have a smooth and uneventful flight. Not sit back and relax…OH, MY GOODNESS!" Silence followed, and after a few minutes, the captain came back on the intercom and said, "Ladies and Gentlemen, I am sorry if I scared you earlier. While I was talking to you, the flight attendant accidentally spilled a cup of hot coffee in my lap. You should see the front of my pants!" A passenger then yelled, "That's nothing. You should see the back of mine!"

WHAT HAS AMERICA BECOME?

Editor,

Has America become the land of the special interest and home of the double standard?

Let's see: if we lie to the Congress, it's a felony and if the Congress lies to us it's just politics: if we dislike a black person, we're racist and if a black dislikes whites, it's their 1st Amendment right; the government spends millions to rehabilitate criminals and they do almost nothing for the victims; in public schools you can teach that homosexuality is OK, but you better not use the word God in the process; you can kill an unborn child, but its wrong to execute a mass murderer; we don't burn books in America, we now rewrite them; we got rid of the communist and socialist threat by renaming them progressives; we are unable to close our border with Mexico, but have no problems protecting the 38th parallel in Korea; if you protest against President Obama's policies you're a terrorist, but if you burned an American flag or George Bush in effigy it was your 1st Amendment right.

You can have pornography on TV or the internet, but you better not put a nativity scene in a public park during Christmas; we have eliminated all criminals in America, they are now called sick people; we can use human fetus for medical research, but it's wrong to use an animal.

We take money from those who work hard for it and give it to those who don't want to work; we all support the Constitution, but only when it supports or political ideology; we still have freedom of speech, but only if we are being politically correct; parenting has been replaced with Ritalin and video games; the land of opportunity is now the land of hand outs; the similarity between Hurricanes and

Katrina and the gulf oil spill is that neither president did anything to help.

And how do we handle a major crisis today? The government appoints a committee to determine who is at fault, then threatens them, passes a law, raises our taxes, tells us the problem is solved so they can get back to their reelection campaign.

What has happened to the land of the free and home of the brave?

Ken Huber
Tawas City

WORKER DEAD AT DESK FOR FIVE DAYS
(IN THE NEW YORK TIMES)

Bosses of a publishing firm are trying to work out why no one noticed that one of their employees had been sitting dead at his desk for five days before anyone asked if he was feeling okay. George Tuklebaum, 51, who had been employed as a proof-reader at a New York firm for 30-years, had a heart attack in the office he shared with 23 other workers.

He quietly passed away on Monday, but nobody noticed until Saturday morning when an office cleaner asked why he was working during the weekend.

His boss, Elliott Wachiaski, said: "George was always the first guy in each morning and the last to leave at night, so no one found it unusual that he was in the same position at the same time and didn't say anything. He was always absorbed in his work and kept much to himself."

A postmortem examination revealed that he had been dead for five days after suffering a fatal coronary. George was proofreading manuscripts of medical textbooks when he died.

You may want to give your co-workers a nudge occasionally. The moral of the story is **don't work too hard. Nobody notices anyway**.

I VOTE FOR LARRY THE CABLE GUY
FOR THE NEXT PRESIDENT

Everyone concentrates on the problems we're having in Our Country lately: Illegal immigration, hurricane recovery, alligators attacking people in Florida.... Not me – I concentrate on solutions for the problems – it's a win-win situation.

- Dig a moat the length of the Mexican border.
- Send the dirt to New Orleans to raise the level of the levees.
- Put the Florida alligators in the moat along the Mexican border.

Think about this: Cows, the Constitution, the Ten Commandments.

- Cows – Is it just me, or does anyone else find it amazing that during the mad cow epidemic our government could track a single cow, born in Canada almost three years ago, right to the stall where she slept in the state of Washington? And, they tracked her calves to their stalls. But they are unable to locate 11 million illegal aliens wandering around our country. Maybe we should give each of them a cow.

- The Constitution – They keep talking about drafting a Constitution for Iraq … why don't we just give them ours? It was written by a lot of really smart guys, it has worked for over 200 years, and we're not using it anymore.

- The Ten Commandments – The real reason that we can't have the Ten Commandments posted in a courthouse is this: You cannot post "Thou Shalt Not Steal", "Thou Shalt Not Commit Adultery" and "Thou Shall Not Lie" in a building full of lawyers, judges and politicians; it creates a hostile work environment.

FOR A GOOD LAUGH
(FOR THE OVER 50 GENERATION)

I thought about the 30 year business I ran with 1800 employees, all without a Blackberry that played music, took videos, pictures and communicated with Facebook and Twitter.

I signed up under duress for Twitter and Facebook, so my seven kids, their spouses, 13 grandchildren and 2 great grandchildren could communicate with grandpa the modern way. I figured I could handle something as simple as Twitter with only 140 characters of space.

That was before one of my grandkids hooked me up for Tweeter, Tweetree, Twirl, Twitterfon, Tweetie and Twittererific Tweetdeck, Twitpix and something that send every message to my cell phone and every other program within the texting world.

My phone was beeping every three minutes with the details of everything except the bowel movements of the entire next generation. I am not ready to live like this. I keep my cell phone in the garage in my golf bag.

The kids bought me a GPS for my last birthday because they say I get lost every now and then going over to the grocery store or library. I keep that in a box under my tool bench with the Blue tooth (its red) phone I am supposed to use when I drive. I wore it once and was standing in line at Barnes and Noble talking to my wife as everyone in the nearest 50 yards was glaring at me. Seems I have to take my hearing aid out to use it, and I got a little loud.

I mean the GPS looked pretty smart on my dashboard, but the lady inside was the most annoying, rudest person I had run into in a long time. Every 10 minutes, she would sarcastically say, "Re-calc-ul-ating route". You would think that she could be nicer. It is like she could barely tolerate me. She would let go with a deep sign and then tell me to make a U-turn at the next light. Then when I would make a right turn instead, it was not good.

When I get really lost now, I call my wife and tell her the name of the cross streets and while she is starting to develop the same tone as Gypsy, the GPS lady, at least she loves me.

To be perfectly frank, I am still trying to learn how to sue the cordless phones in our house. We have them for 4-years, but I still haven't figured out how I can lose three phones all at once and have run around digging under chair cushions and checking bathrooms and the dirty laundry baskets when the phone rings.

The world is just getting to complex for me. They even mess me up every time I go to the grocery store. You would think they could settle on something themselves but this sudden "Paper or Plastic?" every time I check out just knocks me for a loop. I bought some of those cloth reusable bags to avoid looking confused, but I never remember to take them in with me. Now I toss it back to them. When they ask me, "Paper or Plastic?" I just say, "Doesn't matter to me. I am bi-sacksual." Then it's their turn to stare at me with a blank look.

I was recently asked if I tweet. I answered, "No, but I do toot a lot."

PS - I know some of you are not over 50; I sent this to you to allow you to forward it to those who are.

DISORDER IN THE AMERICAN COURTS
(FROM A BOOK BY THE SAME TITLE)

Attorney: What was the first thing your husband said to you that morning?
Witness: He said "Where am I, Cathy?"
Attorney: And why did that upset you?
Witness: My name is Susan!

Attorney: What gear were you in at the moment of impact?
Witness: Gucci sweats and Reeboks.

Attorney: Are you sexually active?
Witness: No, I just lie there.

Attorney: This myasthenia gravis, does it affect your memory at all?
Witness: Yes.
Attorney: And in what ways does it affect your memory?
Witness: I forget.
Attorney: You forget? Can you give us an example of something you forgot?

Attorney: Do you know if your daughter has ever been involved in voodoo?
Witness: We both do.
Attorney: Voodoo?
Witness: We do.
Attorney: You do?
Witness: Yes, voodoo.

Attorney: Now doctor, isn't it true that when a person dies in his sleep, he doesn't know about it until the next morning?

Witness: Did you actually pass the bar exam?

Attorney: The youngest son, the 20-year old, how old is he?
Witness: Are you shitting me?

Attorney: So the date of conception (of the baby) was August 8th?
Witness: Yes.
Attorney: And what were you doing at that time?
Witness: Getting laid!

Attorney: She had three children, right?
Witness: Yes.
Attorney: How many were boys?
Witness: None.
Attorney: Were there any girls?
Witness: Y our Honor, I think I need a different attorney. Can I get a new attorney?

Attorney: How was your first marriage terminated?
Witness: By death.
Attorney: And by whose death was it terminated?
Witness: Take a guess.

Attorney: Can you describe the individual?
Witness: He was about medium height and had a beard.
Attorney: Was this a male or female?
Witness: Unless the Circus was in town I'm going with male.

Attorney: Is your appearance here this morning pursuant to a deposition notice which I sent to your attorney?
Witness: No, this is how I dress when I go to work.

Attorney: Doctor, how many of your autopsies have you performed on dead people?
Witness: All of them. The live ones put up too much of a fight.

Attorney: ALL your responses MUST be oral, OK? What school did you go to?

Witness: Oral.

Attorney: Do you recall the time that you examined the body?

Witness: The autopsy started around 8:30 PM.

Attorney: And Mr. Denton was dead at that time:

Witness: If not, he was by the time I finished.

Attorney: Are you qualified to give a urine sample?

Witness: Are you qualified to as that question?

Attorney: Doctor, before you performed the autopsy, did you check for a pulse?

Witness: No.

Attorney: Did you check for blood pressure?

Witness: No.

Attorney: Did you check for breathing?

Witness: No.

Attorney: So, then it is possible that the patient was alive when you began the autopsy?

Witness: No.

Attorney: How can you be so sure, Doctor?

Witness: Because his brain was sitting on my desk in a jar.

Attorney: I see, but could the patient have still been alive, nevertheless?

Witness: Yes, it is possible that he could have been alive and practicing law.

GRANDMA'S HANDS

Grandma, some ninety plus years, sat feebly on the piano bench. She did't move, just sat there with her head down staring at her hands. When I sat down beside her she didn't acknowledge my presence and the longer I sat there I wondered if she was OK.

Finally, not really wanting to disturb her but wanting to check on her at the same time, I asked her if she was OK. She raised her head and looked at me and smiled. 'Yes, I'm fine, thank you for asking,' she said in a clear voice strong.

'I didn't mean to disturb you, grandma, but you were just sitting here staring at your hands and I wanted to make sure you were OK,' I explained to her.

"Have you ever looked at your hands,' she asked, 'I mean really looked at your hands?'

I slowly opened my hands and stared down at them. I turned them over, palms up and then palms down. I guess I had never really looked at my hands as I tried to figure out the point she was making.

Grandma smiled and related this story:

'Stop and think for a moment about the hands you have, how they have served you well throughout your years. These hands, though wrinkled, shriveled and weak have been the tools I have used all my life to reach out and grab and embrace life.

They put food in my mouth and clothes on my back. As a child, my mother taught me to fold them in prayer. They tied my shoes and pulled on my boots. They held my husband and wiped my tears when he went off to war.

They have been dirty, scraped and raw, swollen and bent. They were uneasy and clumsy when I tried to hold my newborn son. Decorated with my wedding band they showed the world that I was married and loved someone special.

They wrote my letters to him and trembled and shook when I buried my parents and spouse.

They have held my children and grandchildren, consoled neighbors, and shook in fists of anger when I didn't understand.

They have covered my face, combed my hair, and washed and cleansed the rest of my body. They have been sticky and wet, bent and broken, dried and raw. And to this day when not much of anything else of me works real well, these hands hold me up, lay me down, and again continue to fold in prayer.

These hands are the mark of where I've been and ruggedness of life. But more importantly it will be these hands that God will reach out and take when he leads me home. And with my hands He will lift me to His side and there I will use these hands to touch the face of Christ.'

I will never look at my hands the same again. But I remember God reached out and took my grandma's hands and led her home. When my hands are hurt or sore or when I stroke the face of my children and husband, I think of grandma. I know she has been stroked and creased and held by the hand of God.

I, too, want to touch the face of God and feel His hands upon my face.

POSITION

Mom, Mommy, Mama, Ma
Dad, Daddy, Dada, Pa, Pop

JOB DESCRIPTION:

Long term, team players needed, for challenging permanent work in an often chaotic environment. Candidates must possess excellent communications and organizational skills and be willing to work variable hours, which will include evenings and weekends and frequent 24 hour shifts on call …
Some overnight travel required, including trips to primitive camping sites on rainy weekends and endless sports tournaments in far away cities. Travel expenses not reimbursed. Extensive courier duties also required.

RESPONSIBILITIES:

The rest of your life.
Must be willing to be hated, at least temporarily, until someone needs $5.
Must be willing to bite tongue repeatedly.
Also, must possess the physical stamina of a pack mule and be able to go from zero to 60 mph in three seconds flat in case, this time, the screams from the backyard are not someone just crying wolf.
Must be willing to face stimulating technical challenges, such as small gadget repair, mysteriously sluggish toilets and stuck zippers.
Must screen phone calls, maintain calendars and coordinate production of multiple homework projects...

Must have ability to plan and organize social gatherings for clients of all ages and mental outlooks.

Must be willing to be indispensable one minute, and embarrassment the next...

Must handle assembly and product safety testing of a half million cheap, plastic toys, and battery operated devices.

Must always hope for the best but be prepared for the worst.

Must assume final, complete accountability for the quality of the end product.

Responsibilities also include floor maintenance and janitorial work throughout the facility…

POSSIBILITY FOR ADVANCEMENT AND PROMOTION:

None.

Your job is to remain in the same position for years, without complaining, constantly retraining and updating your skills, so that those in your charge can ultimately surpass you.

PREVIOUS EXPERIENCE:

None required unfortunately.

On-the-job training offered on a continually exhausting basis.

WAGES AND COMPENSATION:

Get this! You pay them!

Offering frequent raises and bonuses.

A balloon payment is due when they turn 18 because of the assumption that college will help them become financially independent .

When you die, you give them whatever is left.

The oddest thing about this reverse-salary scheme is that you actually enjoy it and wish you could only do more.

BENEFITS:

While no health or dental insurance, no pension, no tuition reimbursement, no paid holidays and no stock options are offered; this job supplies limitless opportunities for personal growth, unconditional love, and free hugs and kisses for life if you play your cards right.

OFFICIAL NOTICE — FORCED RETIREMENT AT 50!

Due to the current financial situation caused by the slowdown in the economy, Congress has decided to implement a scheme to put workers of 50 years of age and above on early retirement, thus creating jobs and reducing unemployment.

This scheme will be known as RAPE (Retired Aged People Early)

Persons selected to be RAPED can apply to Congress to be considered for the SHAFT program (Special Help After Forced Termination).

Persons who have been RAPED and SHAFTED will be reviewed under the SCREW program (System Covering Retired-Early Workers).

A person may be RAPED once, SHAFTED twice and SCREWED as many times as Congress deems appropriate.

Persons who have been RAPED could get AIDS (Additional Income for Dependent & Spouse) or HERPES (Half Earnings for Retired Personnel Early Severance).

Obviously persons who have AIDS or HERPES will not be SHAFTED or SCREWED any further by Congress.

Persons who are not RAPED and are staying on will receive as much SHIT (Special High Intensity Training) as possible. Congress has always prided themselves on the amount of SHIT they give our citizens.

Should you feel that you do not receive enough SHIT, please bring this to the attention of your Congressman, who has been trained to give you all the SHIT you can handle.

Sincerely,
The Committee for Economic Value of Individual Lives (E.V.I.L.)
Ben Dover, Chrmn.

P.S. - Due to recent budget cuts and the rising cost of electricity, gas and oil, as well as current market conditions, the Light at the End of the Tunnel has been turned off.

COLONOSCOPY JOURNAL

I called my friend Andy Sable, a gastroenterologist, to make an appointment for a colonoscopy.

A few days later, in his office, Andy showed me a color diagram of the colon, a lengthy organ that appears to go all over the place, at one point passing briefly through Minneapolis.

Then Andy explained the colonoscopy procedure to me in a thorough, reassuring and patient manner.

I nodded thoughtfully, but I didn't really hear anything he said, because my brain was shrieking, "HE'S GOING TO STICK A TUBE 17,000 FEET UP YOUR BEHIND!"

I left Andy's office with some written instructions, and a prescription for a product called 'MoviPrep', which comes in a box large enough to hold a microwave oven. I will discuss MovePred in detail later; for now suffice it to say that we must never allow it to fall into the hands of America's enemies.

I spent the next several days productively sitting around being nervous.

Then, on the day before my colonoscopy, I began my preparation. In accordance with my instructions, I didn't eat any solid food that day; all I had was chicken broth, which is basically water, only with less flavor.

Then, in the evening, I took the MoviPrep. You mix two packets of power together in a one-liter plastic jug, and then you fill it with lukewarm water. (For those unfamiliar with the metric system, a liter is about 32 gallons) Then you have to drink the whole jug. This takes about an hour, because MoviPrep tastes – and her I am being kind – like a mixture of goat spit and urinal cleanser, with just a hint of lemon.

This is kind of like saying that after you jump off your roof, you may experience contact with the ground.

MoviPrep is a nuclear laxative. I don't want to be too graphic, here, but, have you ever seen a space-shuttle launch?

This is pretty much the MoviPrep experience, with you as the shuttle. There are times when you wish the commode had a seat belt. You spend several hours pretty much confined to the bathroom, spurting violently. You eliminate everything. And then, when you figure you must be totally empty, you have to drink another liter of MoviPrep, at which point, as far as I can tell, your bowels travel into the future and start eliminating food that you have not even eaten yet.

After an action-packed evening, I finally got to sleep.

The next morning my love drove me to the clinic I was very nervous. Not only was I worried about the procedure, but I had been experiencing occasional return bouts of MoviPrep spurtage. I was thinking, 'What if I spurt on Andy?' How do you apologize to a friend for something like that? Flowers would not be enough.

At the clinic I had to sign many forms acknowledging that I understood and totally agreed with whatever the heck the forms said. Then they led me to a room full of other colonoscopy people, where I went inside a little curtained space and took off my clothes and put on one of those hospital garments designed by sadist perverts, the kind that, when you put it on, makes you feel even more naked than when you are actually naked.

Then a nurse named Eddie put a little needle in a vein in my left hand. Ordinarily I would have fainted, but Eddie was very good, and I was already lying down. Eddie also told me that some people put vodka in their MoviPrep. At first I was ticked off that I hadn't thought of this, but then I pondered what would happen if you got yourself too tipsy to make it to the bathroom, so you were staggering around in full Fire House Mode.

You would have no choice burn to burn your house.

When everything was ready, Eddie wheeled me into the procedure room, where Andy was waiting with a nurse and an anesthesiologist. I did not see the 17,000-foot tube, but I knew Andy had it hidden around there somewhere. I was seriously nervous at this point.

Andy had me rollover on my left side, and the anesthesiologist began hooking something up to the needle in my hand.

There was music playing in the room, and I realized that the song was 'Dancing Queen' by ABBA. I remarked to Andy that, all of the songs that could be playing during this particular procedure, 'Dancing Queen' had to be the least appropriate.

'You want me to turn it up?' said Andy, from somewhere behind me.

'Ha ha,' I said. And then it was time, the moment I had been dreading for more than a decade. If you are squeamish, prepare yourself, because I am going to tell you, in explicit detail, exactly what it was like.

I have no idea .. Really. I slept through it. One moment, ABBA was yelling 'Dancing Queen, feel the beat of the tambourine,' and the next moment, I was back in the other room, waking up in a very mellow mood.

Andy was looking down at me and asking me how I felt. I felt excellent. I felt even more excellent when Andy told me that it was all over, and that my colon had passed with flying colors. I have never been prouder of an internal organ.

On the subject of colonoscopies …
Colonoscopies are no joke, but these comments during the exam were quite humorous …A physician claimed that the following are actual comments made by his patients predominately male) while he was performing their colonoscopies:

1. 'Take it easy, Doc. You're boldly going where no man has gone before!'
2. 'Find Amelia Earhart yet?'
3. 'Can you hear me NOW?'
4. 'Are we there yet? Are we there yet? Are we there yet?'
5. 'You know, in Arkansas, we're now legally married.'
6. 'Any sign of the trapped miners, Chief?'
7. 'You put your left hand in, you take your left hand out …'
8. 'Hey Doc, let me know if you find my dignity ..'
9. 'If your hand doesn't fit, you must quit!'
10. 'Hey! Now I know how a Muppet feels!'
11. 'You used to be an executive at Enron, didn't you?'
12. 'God, now I know why I am not gay.'

<u>And the best one of all:</u>

13. 'Could you write a note for my wife saying that my head is not up there?'

ORANGES

Lulu was a prostitute, but she didn't want her grandma to know. One day, the police raided the brothel and took all the girls outside and made them line up. Suddenly, Lulu's grandma came by.

Grandma asked, "Why are you standing in line here dear?" Not willing to let her grandma know the truth, Lulu told her that the police were passing out free oranges and she was just lining up for some.

"Why, that's awfully nice of them. I think I'll get some for myself," Grandma said, and she proceeded to the end of the line.

A policeman was going down the line asking for information from all the prostitutes. When he got to Grandma he was bewildered and exclaimed, "Wow, still going at it at your age? How do you do it?" Grandma replied, "Oh, it's easy, dear. I just take my dentures out, rip the skin back and suck 'em' dry."

The policeman fainted.

HE SAID TO ME!

He said to me … I don't know why you wear a bra; you've got nothing to put in it. I said to him … You wear paints don't you?

He said to me … Shall we try swapping positions tonight? I said, that's a good idea – you stand by the stove and sink while I sit on the sofa and do nothing but break wind.

He said to me … What have you been doing with all the grocery money I gave you? I said to him … Turn sideways and look in the mirror!

He said to me … Why don't women blink during foreplay? I said to him … They don't have time.

He said to me … How many men does it take to change a roll of toilet paper? I said to him … I don't know; it has never happened.

 He said to me … Why is it difficult to find men who are sensitive, caring and Good-looking? I said to him … They already have boyfriends. He said … What do you call a woman who knows where her husband is every night? I said … A widow.

He said to me … Why are married women heavier than single women? I said to him … Single women come home, see what's in the fridge and go to bed. Married women come home, see what's in bed and go to the fridge.

ANGER MANAGEMENT

When you occasionally have a really bad day, and you just need to take it out on someone, don't take it out on someone you know, take it out on someone you don't know, but you know deserves it.

I was sitting at my desk when I remembered a phone call I'd forgotten to make...I found the number and dialed it.

A man answered, saying 'Hello.'

I politely said, 'This is Chris. Could I please speak with Robyn Carter?'

Suddenly a manic voice yelled out in my ear 'Get the right F***ing number!' And the phone was slammed down on me.

I couldn't believe that anyone could be so rude.

When I tracked down Robyn's correct number to call her, I found that I had accidentally transposed the last two digits.

After hanging up with her, I decided to call the 'wrong' number again. When the same guy answered the phone, I yelled 'You're an asshole!' And hung up. I wrote his number down with the word 'asshole' next to it , and put it in my desk drawer.

Every couple of weeks, when I was paying bills or had a really bad day, I'd call him up and yell, 'You're an asshole!' It always cheered me up.

When Caller ID was introduced, I thought my therapeutic 'asshole' calling would have to stop. So, I called his number and said, "Hi, this is John Smith from the telephone company. I'm calling to see if you're familiar with our Called ID Program?"

He yelled "No!" And slammed down the phone. I quickly called him back and said, "that's because you're an asshole!" And hung up.

One day I was at the store, getting ready to pull into a parking spot. Some guy in a black BMW cut me off and pulled into the spot I had patiently waited for. I hit the horn and yelled that I'd been waiting for that spot, but the idiot ignored me.

I notice a "For Sale" sign in his back window, so I wrote down his number. A couple days later, right after calling the first asshole (I had his number on speed dial) I thought that I'd better cal the BMW asshole, too.

I said "Is this the man with the black BMW for sale?" He said "Yes, it is". I then asked "Can you tell me where I can see it?" He said, "Yes, I live a 34 Oaktree Blvd., in Fairfax it's a yellow ranch style house and the car's parked right out in front."

I asked, What's your name?" He said "My name is Don Hansen." I asked, "When's a good time to catch you, Don?" He said "I'm home every evening after five." I said "Listen, Don, can I tell you something?" He said, "Yes". I said "Don, you're as asshole!" Then I hung up, and added his number to my speed dial, too.

Now, when I had a problem, I had two assholes to call. Then I came up with an idea…I called asshole #1. He said "Hello". I said "You're as asshole!" (But did not hang up).
He asked, "Are you still there?" I said "Yeah!"

He screamed, "Stop calling me". I said, "Make me." He asked, "Who are you?" I said my name is Dan Hansen." He said, "Yeah? Where do you live". I said, "Asshole, I live at 34 Oaktree Blvd., in Fairfax, a yellow ranch style home and I have a black Beamer parked in front".

He said, "I'm coming over right now, Don. And you had better start saying your prayers." I said, "Yeah, like I'm really scared, asshole."

Then I called Asshole #2. He said, "Hello?" I said, "Hello, asshole." He yelled, "If I ever find out who you are…" I said, "You'll what?" He exclaimed, "I'll kick your ass".

I answered, "Well, asshole, here's your chance…I'm coming over right now." Then I hung up and immediately called the police, saying that I was on my way over to 34 Oaktree Blvd., Fairfax, to kill my gay lover.

Then I called Channel 7 News about the gang war going down on Oaktree Blvd. in Fairfax. I quickly got into my car and headed over to Fairfax.

I got there just in time to watch two assholes beating the crap out of each other in front of six cop cars, an overhead news helicopter and surrounded by a news crew.

NOW I feel much better.

Anger management really does work!

DADDY, HOW WAS I BORN?

A little boy goes to his father and asks "Daddy, how was I born?"

The father answers, "Well, son, I guess one day you will need to find our anyway! Your mom and I first got together in a chat room on Yahoo. Then I set up a date via e-mail with your Mom and we met at a cyber-café. We sneaked into a secluded room, and googled each other. There your mother agreed to a download from my hard drive. As soon as I was ready to upload, we discovered that neither on of us had used a firewall, and since it was too late to hit the delete button, nine months later a little pop-up appeared that said: "You got MALE!"

LIFE IS ALL ABOUT ASSES

You're either covering it,
Laughing it off,
Kicking it,
Kissing it,
Busting it,
Trying to get a piece of it,
Or behaving like one.

WHAT IS A GRANDPARENT?

Taken from papers written by a class of 8-year-olds. You'll love it:

- Grandparents are a lady and a man who have no little children of their own. They like other peoples.

- A grandfather is a man & a grandmother is a lady!

- Grandparents don't have to do anything except be there when we come to see them. They are so old they shouldn't play hard or run. It is good if they drive us to the shops and give us money.

- When they take us for walks, they slow down past things like pretty leaves and caterpillars.

- They show us and talk to us about the colors of the flowers and also why we shouldn't step on 'cracks'.

- They don't hurry up.

- Usually grandmothers are fat but not too fat to tie your shoes.

- They wear glasses and funny underwear.

- They can take their teeth and gums out.

- Grandparents don't have to be smart.

- They have to answer questions like 'Why isn't God married?' and how come dogs chase cats?

- When they read to us, they don't skip. They don't mind if we ask for the same story over again.

- Everybody should try to have a grandmother, especially if you don't have television because they are the only grownups who like to spend time with us.

- They know we should have snack time before bed time, and they say prayers with us and kiss us even when we've acted bad.

- It's funny when they bend over, you hear gas leaks, and they blame the dog.'

A 6-year old was asked where his grandma lived, "Oh, she lives at the airport, and when we want her, we just go get her. Then when we're done having her visit, we take her back to the airport."

Grandpa is the smartest man on earth! He teaches me good things, but I don't get to see him enough to get as smart as him!

INNER PEACE

If you can start the day without caffeine,
If you can always be cheerful, ignoring aches and pains,
If you can resist complaining and boring people with your troubles,
If you can eat the same food every day and be grateful for it,
If you can understand when your loved ones are too busy to give you any time,
If you can take criticism and blame without resentment,
If you can conquer tension without medical help,
If you can relax without a glass of wine,
If you can sleep without the aid of drugs,

…Then You Are Probably

…The family dog.

And you thought I was going to get all spiritual.

EYE-TALIAN

Why do Italians hate Jehovah's Witnesses?
Because Italians hate all witnesses.

Do you know why most men from Italy are named Tony?

On the boat over to America they put a sticker on them that said TO NY (To New York).

You know you're Italian when….
You can bench press 325 pounds, shave twice a day and still cry when your mother yells at you.

You carry your lunch in a produce bag because you can't fit two cappicola sandwiches, 4 oranges, 2 bananas and pizzelles into a regular lunch bag.

Your mechanic, plumber, electrician, accountant, travel agent and lawyer are all your cousins.

You have at least 5 cousins living in the same town or on the same block. All five of those cousins are named after your grandfather or grandmother.

You are on a first name basis with at least 8 banquet hall owners.

You only get one good shave from a disposable razor.

If someone in your family grows beyond 5'9", it is presumed his Mother had an affair.

There were more than 28 people in your bridal party.

You netted more than $50,000 on your first communion.

And you REALLY, REALLY know your Italian when…

Your grandfather had a fig tree.

You eat Sunday dinner at 2:00.

Christmas Eve…only fish.

Your mom's meatballs are the best balls.

You've been hit with a wooden spoon or had a shoe thrown at you.

Clear plastic covers on all the furniture.

You know how to pronounce 'manicotti" and "mozzarella."

You fight over whether it's called 'sauce" or "gravy".

You've called someone a "mamaluke".

And you understand "bada bing".

Italians have a $40,000 kitchen, but use the $259 stove from Sears in the basement to cook.

There is some sort of religious statue in the hallway, living room, bedroom, front porch and backyard.

The living room is filled with old wedding favors with poofy net bows and stale almonds (they are too pretty to open).

A portrait of the Pope and Frank Sinatra hang in the dining room.

God forbid if anyone EVER attempted to eat 'ChefBoy-ar-dee', 'Franco American', 'Ragu'. 'Prego', or anything else labeled as Italian in a jar or can.

Meatballs are made with pork, veal and beef. Italians do not care about cholesterol.

Turkey is served on Thanksgiving AFTER the manicotti, gnocchi, lasagna, and minestrone or escarole soup.

If anyone EVER says ESCAROLE, slap 'em in the face – it's SHCAROLE.

Sunday dinner was at 1:00 PM sharp. The meal went like this…The table was set with everyday dishes. It doesn't matter if they don't match. They're clean; what more do you want?

All the utensils go on the right side of the plate and the napkin goes on the left.

A clean kitchen towel was put at Nonna's & Papa's plates because they won't use napkins.

Homemade wine and bottles of 7up are on the table.

First course, Antipasto…..change plates.

Second course, macaroni. All pasta was called macaroni…..change plates.

Third course, roast beef, potatoes and vegetables…..change plates.

THEN, and only then – NEVER AT THE BEGINNING OF THE MEAL – would you eat the salad drenched in homemade oil & vinegar dressing…..change plates.

Next course, fruit & nuts – in the shell – on paper plates because you ran out of the real ones.

Last was coffee with anisette. Espresso for Nonna, 'American' coffee for the rest with hard cookies (biscotti) to dunk in the coffee.

The kids would go out to play.

The men would go lay down. They slept so soundly that you could do brain surgery on them without anesthesia.

The women cleaned the kitchen.

We got screamed at my Mom or Nonna, and half of the sentences were English, the other half Italian.

Italian mothers never threw a baseball in their life, but could nail you in the head with a shoe thrown from the kitchen while you were in the living room.

Other things particular to Italians….

The prom dress that Zia Ceserina made you cost only $20.00, which was for the material.

The prom hairdo was done free by Cousin Angela.

Turning around at the prom to see your entire family, including you Godparents, standing in the back of the gym…..PRICELESS !

True Italians will love this.

Those of you who are married to Italians will understand this.

And those who wish they were Italian, and those who are friends with Italians, will remember with a smile.

O.M.G., I'M RICH!

Silver in the Hair
Gold in the Teeth
Sugar in the Blood
Crystals in the Kidneys
Lead in the Ass
Iron in the Arteries
And…an inexhaustible supply of Natural Gas

I never thought I'd accumulate such wealth.

THE QUEEN AND DOLLY GO TO HEAVEN

Queen Elizabeth and Dolly Parton die on the same day and they both go before an Angel to find out if they'll be admitted to Heaven. Unfortunately, there's only one space left that day, so the Angel must decide which of them gets in. The Angel asks Dolly if there's some particular reason why she should go to Heaven.

Dolly takes off her tip and says, "look at these, they're the most perfect breasts God ever created, and I'm sure it will please God to be able to see them every day, for eternity."

The Angel thanks Dolly, and asks Her Majesty the same question. The Queen takes a bottle of Perrier out of her purse, drinks it down. Then, wees into a toilet and pulls the lever. The Angel says, "OK, your Majesty, you may go in."

Dolly is outraged and asks, "What was that all about? I show you two of God's own perfect creations and you turn me down. She wees into a toilet and she gets in! Would you explain that to me?"

"Sorry, Dolly," says the Angel, "but even in Heaven, A Royal Flush, beats a Pair - No matter how big they are.

CONGRESSMAN

A congressman was seated next to a little girl on an airplane so he turned to her and said, "Do you want to talk? Flights go quicker if you strike up a conversation with your fellow passenger."

The little girl, who had just started to read her book, replied to the total stranger, "What would you want to talk about"?

"Oh, I don't know," said the congressman. "How about global warming, universal health care, or stimulus packages?" as he smiled smugly.

"PK," she said. "Those could be interesting topics but let me ask you a question first. A horse, a cow, and a deer all eat the same stuff – grass. Yet a deer excretes little pellets, while a cow turns out a flat patty, but a horse produces clumps. Why do you suppose that is?"

The legislator, visibly surprised by the little girl's intelligence, thinks about it and says, "Hmmm, I have no idea."

To which the little girl replies, "Do you really feel qualified to discuss global warming, universal health care, or the economy, when you don't know shit?" And then she went back to reading her book.

HATS OFF TO THE ISRAELIS!

FINALLY – A great alternative to body scanners at airports.

The Israelis are developing an airport security device that eliminates the privacy concerns that come with full-body scanners at the airports.

It's a booth you can step into that will not X-ray you, but will detonate any explosive device you may have on you. They see this as a win-win for everyone, with none of this crap about racial profiling. It also would eliminate the costs of a long and expensive trial. Justice would be swift. Case closed!

You're in the airport terminal and you hear a muffled explosion. Shortly thereafter an announcement comes over the PA system…"Attention standby passengers - we now have a seat available on flight number 1234. Shalom!"

WOMEN'S PLACE IN THIS WORLD

I knew the day would come when men had an answer to Maxine. Next, Marvin, men's answer to Maxine.

1. Her job is to bitch…mine is to giver her a reason!

2. How many men does it take to open a beer? None. It should be opened when she brings it.

3. Why is a Laundromat a really bad place to pick up a woman? Because a woman who can't even afford a washing machine will probably never be able to support you.

4. Why do women have smaller feet than men? It's one of those 'evolutionary things' that allows them to stand closer to the kitchen sink.

5. How do you know when a woman is about to say something smart? When she starts a sentence with 'A man once told me.'

6. How do you fix a woman's watch? You don't. There is a clock on the oven.

7. If your dog is barking at the back door and your wife is yelling at the front door, who do you let in first? The dog, of course. He'll shut up once you let him in.

8. Scientists have discovered a food that diminishes a woman's sex drive by 90%. It's called a Wedding Cake.

9. Why do men die before their wives? They want to.

10. Women will never be equal to men, until they can walk down the street with a bald head and a beer gut, and still think they are sexy.

11. Maxine just had to have the last word. Wipe your mouth, there's still a tiny bit of bullshit around your lips.

JUST A NOTE

Just think....if the Indians had given the Pilgrims a donkey instead of a turkey, we would all be having a piece of ass this Thanksgiving !!

ERIC FIXED MY COMPUTER

As we Silver Surfers know, sometimes we have trouble with our computers.

I had a problem yesterday, so I called Eric, the 13 year old next door, whose bedroom looks like Mission Control, and asked him to come over.

Eric clicked a couple of buttons and solved the problem. As he was walking away, I called after him, 'So, what was wrong?'

He replied, 'It was an ID ten T error.' I didn't want to appear stupid, but nonetheless inquired. 'An, ID ten T error? What's that? In case I need to fix it again.'

Eric grinned...'Haven't you ever heard of an ID ten T error before?' 'No,' I replied.

'Write it down', he said, 'and I think you'll figure it out.' So I wrote down:

ID10T

I use to like Eric, the little bastard.

A GLASS OF WINE

To all my friends who enjoy a glass of wine…And those who don't and are always seen with a bottle of water in their hand.

As Ben Franklin said, "In wine there is wisdom, in beer there is freedom, in water there is bacteria."

In a number of carefully controlled trials, Scientists have demonstrated that if we drink 1 liter of water each day, at the end of the year we would have absorbed more than 1 kilo of Escherichia coli, (E..Coli) – bacteria bound in feces. In other words, we are consuming 1 kilo of poop.

However, we do NOT run that risk when drinking wine, beer, tequila, rum, whiskey, or other liquor. Because alcohol has to go through a purification process of boiling, filtering and/or fermenting.

Remember: water = poop, wine = health.

Therefore, it is better to drink wine and talk stupid, than to drink water and be full of shit.
(There is no need to thank me for this valuable information: I'm doing it as a public service!)

ITALIAN GRANDMA'S ADVICE

A young Italian girl was going on a date. Her Nonna said: "Sita here ana letame tella you about this-a younga boy. He's agonna try ana kiss you, you are agonna likea dat, but don't let him do dat.

He's agonna try ana kiss your breasts, you are agonna likea dat too, but don'ta let him do dat eeda.

But mosta important, he's agonna try ana lay a topa you, you are agonna really lika dat, but don'ta let him do dat for sure. Doing thata willa disgraza our family.

With that bit of advise, the granddaughter went on her date. The next day she tolk grandma that her date went just like she had predicted. "And Nonna, I didn't let him disgrace our family as you said. When he tried to lay on top of me, I just rolled him over, got on top of him, and disgraced HIS family!"

Grandma fainted.

MY LAST TRIP TO COSTCO

Yesterday I was at my local Costco buying a large bag of Purina dog show for my loyal pet, Jake, the Wonder Dog, and was in the check-out line when a woman behind me asked if I had a dog.

What did she think I had, an elephant? So since I'm retired and have little to do, on impulse I told her that no, I didn't have a dog, I was starting the Purina Diet again. I added that I probably shouldn't, because I ended up in the hospital last time, but that I'd lost 50 pounds before I awakened in an intensive care ward with tubes coming out of most of my orifices and IV's in both arms.

I told her that it was essentially a perfect diet and that the way that it works is, to load your pants pockets with Purina Nuggets and simply eat one or two every time you feel hungry. The food is nutritionally complete, so it works well and I was going to try it again. (I have to mention here that practically everyone in line was not enthralled with my story.)

Horrified, she asked if I ended up in intensive care, because the dog food poisoned me. I told her no, I stepped off a curb to sniff a poodle's ass and a car hit me. I thought the guy behind her was going to have a heart attack he was laughing so hard.

2011

ADULT TRUTHS

1. I think part of best friend's job should be to immediately clear your computer history if you die.

2. Nothing sucks more than that moment during an argument when you realize you're wrong.

3. I totally take back all those times I didn't want to nap when I was younger.

4. There is great need for a sarcasm front.

5. How the hell are you supposed to fold a fitted sheet?

6. Was learning cursive really necessary?

7. Map Quest really needs to start their directions on #5. I'm pretty sure I know how to get out of my neighborhood.

8. Obituaries would be a lot more interesting if they told you how the person died.

9. I can't remember the last time I wasn't at least kind of tired.

10. Bad decisions make good stories.

11. You never know when it will strike, but there comes a moment at work when you know that you just aren't going to do anything productive for the rest of the day.

12. Can we all just agree to ignore whatever comes after Blue Ray? I don't want to restart my collection…again.

13. I'm always slightly terrified when I exit our of Word and it asks me if I want to save any changes to my ten-page technical report that I swear I did not make any changes to.

14. I keep some people's phone numbers in my phone just so I know not to answer when they call.

15. I think the freezer deserves a light as well.

16. I disagree with Kay Jewelers, I would bet on any given Friday or Saturday night more kisses begin with alcohol than Kay.

17. I wish Google Maps had an "Avoid Ghetto" routing option.

18. I have a hard time deciphering the fine line between boredom and hunger.

19. How many times is it appropriate to say "What?" before you just not and smile because you still didn't hear or understand a word they said?

20. I love the sense of camaraderie when an entire line of cars team up to prevent a jerk from cutting in at the front. Stay strong, brothers and sisters!

21. Shirts get dirty. Underwear gets dirty. Pants? Pants never get dirty, and you can wear them forever.

22. Sometimes I'll look down at my watch 3 consecutive times and still not know what time it is.

23. Even under ideal conditions people have trouble locating their car keys in a pocket, finding their cell phone, and Pinning the Tail on the Donkey – but I'd bet everyone can find and push the snooze button from 3 feet away, in about 1.7 seconds, eyes closed, first time, every time.

SENIOR HEALTH CARE SOLUTION
ACCORDING TO MAXINE

So you're a sick senior citizen and the government says there is no nursing home available for you – what do you do?

Our plan gives anyone 65 years or older a gun and 4 bullets. You are allowed to shoot 4 politicians – not necessarily dead!

Of course, this means you will be sent to prison where you will get 3 meals a day, a roof over your head, central heating and air conditioning, and all the health care you need! New teeth – no problem. Need glasses, great. New hip replacement, knees, lungs, heart? All covered. (And your kids can come and visit you as often as they do now).

And who will be paying for all of this? The same government that just told you that they cannot afford for you to go into t nursing home. Plus, because you are a prisoner, you don't have to pay any income taxes anymore. IS THIS A GREAT COUNTRY OR WHAT?

FOUR BROTHERS' GIFT TO THEIR MOTHER

Four brothers left home for college, and they became successful doctors and lawyers and prospered. Some years later, they chatted after having dinner together. They discussed the gifts they were able to give their elderly mother who lived far away in another city.

The first said, "I had a big house built for Mamma."

The second said, "I had a hundred thousand dollar theater built in the house."

The third said, "I had my Mercedes dealer deliver an SL600 to her."

The fourth said, "You know how Mama loved reading the Bible and you know she can't read anymore because she can't see very well. I met this preacher who told me about a parrot that can recite the entire Bible. It took twenty preachers 12 years to teach him. I had to pledge to contribute $50,000 a year for twenty years to the church, but it was worth it. Mama just has to name the chapter and verse and the parrot will recite it."

The other brothers were impressed. After the holidays Mom sent out her Thank You notes.

She wrote: "Milton, the house you built is so huge that I live in only one room, but I have to clean the whole house. Thanks anyway."
"Marvin, I am too old to travel. I stay home, I have my groceries delivered, so I never use the Mercedes. But. I do appreciate the thought. Thanks."

"Michael, you gave me an expensive theater with Dolby sound, but I've lost my hearing and I'm nearly blind. I'll never use it. But, thank you for the gesture just the same."

"Dearest Melvin, you were the only son to have the good sense to give a little thought to your gift. The chicken was delicious. Thank you."

Love,
Mama

WRONG E-MAIL ADDRESS

This one is priceless…A lesson to be learned from typing the wrong email address!!

A Minneapolis couple decided to go to Florida to Thaw out during a particularly icy winter. They planned to stay at the same hotel where they spent their honeymoon 20 years earlier.

Because of hectic schedules, it was difficult to coordinate their travel schedules. So, the husband left Minnesota and flew to Florida on Thursday, with his wife flying down the following day.

The husband checked into the hotel. There was a computer in his room, so he decided to send an email to his wife. However, he accidentally left out one letter in her email address, and without realizing his error, sent the email.

Meanwhile, somewhere in Houston, a widow had just returned home from her husband's funeral. He was a minister who was called home to glory following a heart attack.

The widow decided to check her email expecting messages from relatives and friends. After reading the first message, she screamed and fainted.

The widow's son rushed into the room, found his mother on the floor, and saw the computer screen which read:
To: My loving wife
Subject: I've arrived
Date: October 16, 2010

I know you're surprised to hear from me. They have computers here now and you are allowed to send emails to your loved ones. I've just arrived and have been checked in.

I've seen that everything has been prepared for your arrival tomorrow. Looking forward to seeing you then!! Hope your journey is as uneventful as mine.

P.S. - Sure is freaking hot down here!

THE PRINCE AND THE PRINCESS

Once upon a time, a Prince asked a beautiful Princess, "Will you marry me?" The Princess said, "NO!!!" And the Prince lived happily ever after and rode motorcycles and banged skinny long-legged big-tittie broads and hunted and fished and raced cars and went to naked bars and dated women half his age and drank whiskey, beer and Captain Morgan and never heard bitching and never paid child support or alimony and banged cheerleaders and kept his house and guns and ate spam and potato chips and beans and blew enormous farts and never got cheated on while he was at work and all his friends and family thought he was cool as hell and he had tons of money in the bank and left the toilet seat up.

The End.

JEFF GORDON FIRES PIT CREW

Raleigh, NC.

Jeff Gordon announced today that he was firing his entire pit crew. This announcement followed Gordon's decision to take advantage of President Obama's scheme to employ Harlem youngsters. The decision to hire them was brought about by a recent documentary on how unemployed youths from Harlem were able to remove a set of wheels in less than 6 seconds without proper equipment, whereas Gordon's existing crew could only do it in 8 seconds with thousands of dollars worth of high tech equipment.

It was thought to be an excellent and bold move by Gordon's management team, as most races are won or lost in the pits. However, Gordon got more than he bargained for.

At the crew's first practice session, not only was the inexperience crew able to change all 4 wheels in under 6 seconds, but within 12 seconds they had changed the paint scheme, altered the VIN number, and sold the car to Kyle Busch for 10 cases of Bud, a bag of weed, and some photos of Jeff Gordon's wife in the shower.

RALPH AND EDNA

Just because someone doesn't love you the way you want them to, doesn't mean they don't love you with all they have.

Ralph and Edna were both patients in a mental hospital. One day while they were walking past the hospital swimming pool, Ralph suddenly jumped into the deep end.
He sank to the bottom of the pool and stayed there.

Edna promptly jumped in to save him. She swam to the bottom and pulled him out. When the Head Nurse Director became aware of Edna's heroic act she immediately ordered her to be discharged from the hospital, as she now considered her to be mentally stable.

When she went to tell Edna the news she said, "Edna, I have good news and bad news. The good news is you are being discharged, since you were able to rationally respond to a crisis by jumping in and saving the life of the person you love. I have concluded that your act displays sound mindedness. The bad news is Ralph hung himself in the bathroom with his bathrobe belt right after you saved him. I am sorry, but he is dead."

Edna replied, "He didn't hang himself. I put him there to dry…. How soon can I go home?"

AN AMAZING MAN

A man walked out to the street and caught a taxi just going by. He got into the taxi, and the cabbie said, "Perfect timing. You're just like Brian."

Passenger: "Who."

Cabbie: "Brian. He's a guy who did everything right all the time. Like my coming along when you needed a cab, things happen like that to Brian, every single time."

Passenger: "There are always a few clouds over everybody."

Cabbie: "Not Brian. He was a terrific athlete. He could have won the Grand Slam at tennis. He could golf with the pros. HE sang like an opera baritone and danced like a Broadway star and you should have heard him play the piano. He was an amazing guy."

Passenger: "Sounds like he was something really special."

Cabbie: "There's more. He had a memory like a computer. He remembered everybody's birthday. He knew all about wines, which foods to order and which fork to eat them with. He could fix anything. Not like me. I change a fuse, and the whole street blacks out. But Brian, he could do everything right."

Passenger: "Wow, some guy then."

Cabbie: "He always knew the quickest way to go in traffic and avoid traffic jams. Not like me, I always seem to get stuck in them. But Brian, he never made a mistake, and he really knew how to treat a woman and make her feel good. HE would never answer her back even if she was in the wrong; and his clothing was always immaculate, shoes highly polished too. HE was the perfect man! He never made a mistake. No one could ever measure up to Brian…"

Passenger: "An amazing fellow. How did you meet him?"

Cabbie: "Oh, I never actually met Brian. He died. I'm married to his fucking widow.

WALK NAKED IN AMERICA DAY

Don't forget to mark your calendars. As you may already know, it is a sin for a Muslim male to see any woman other than his wife naked, and if he does, he must commit suicide.

So next Saturday, at 1 p.m. Eastern Time, all American women are asked to walk naked for one hour.

THE PATIENT GRANDFATHER

A woman in a supermarket is following a grandfather and his badly behaved 3 year-old grandson. It's obvious to her that he has his hands full with the child screaming for sweets in the sweet isle, biscuits in the biscuit aisle, and for fruit, cereal and pop in the other aisles. Meanwhile, Gramps is working his way around, saying in a controlled voice, "Easy, William, we won't be long … easy, boy."

Another outburst, and she hears the granddad calmly say, "It's okay William, just a couple more minutes and we'll be out of here. Hang in there. Boy."

At the checkout, the little terror is throwing items out of the cart, and Gramps says again in a controlled voice, "William, William, relax buddy, don't get upset. We'll be home in five minutes; stay cool, William."

Very impressed, the woman goes outside where the grandfather is loading his groceries and the boy into the car. She said to the elderly gentleman, "It's none of my business, but you were amazing in there. I don't know how you do it. That whole time, you kept your composure, and no matter how loud and disruptive he got, you just calmly kept saying things would be okay. William is very lucky to have you as his grandpa."

"Thanks lady," said the grandfather, "but I'm William … the little shit's name is Steve."

SEX AFTER DEATH

A couple made a deal that whoever died first would come back and inform the other of the afterlife. Their biggest fear was that there was no after life at all. After a long life together, the husband was the first to die. True to his word, he made the first contact.

"Marion...Marion..."

"Is that you, Bob?"

"Yes, I've come back like we agreed."

"That's wonderful! What's it like?"

"Well, I get up in the morning, I have sex. I have breakfast and then it's off to the golf course. I have sex again, bathe in the warm sun and then have sex a couple more times. Then I have lunch (you'd be proud – lots of greens). Another romp around the golf course, then pretty much have sex the rest of the afternoon. After supper, it's back to golf course again. Then it's more sex until late at night. I catch some much needed sleep and then the next day it starts all over again."

"Oh, Bob are you in heaven?"

"No...I'm a rabbit in Arizona!"

MAKE YOU SMILE

If this doesn't make you laugh…you are having a really bad day!!!

A guy is driving around the back woods of Montana and he sees a sign in front of a broken down shanty-style house: "Talking Dog For Sale". He rings the bell and the owner appears and tells him the dog is in the backyard.

The guy goes into the backyard and sees a nice looking Labrador Retriever sitting there.

"You talk?" he asks.

"Yep," the Lab replies.

After the guy recovers from the shock of hearing a dog talk, he says, "So, what's your story?"

The Lab looks up and says, "Well, I discovered that I could talk when I was pretty young. I wanted to help the government, so I told the CIA. In no time at all they had me jetting from country to country, sitting in rooms with spies and world leaders, because no one figured a dog would be eavesdropping." I was one of their most valuable spies for eight years running. But the jetting around really tired me out, and I knew I wasn't getting any
Younger so I decided to settle down. I signed up for a job at the airport to do some undercover security, wandering near suspicious characters and listening in. I uncovered some incredible dealings and was awarded a batch of medals. I got married, had a mess of puppies, and now I'm just retired."

This guy is amazed. He goes back in and asks the owner what he wants for the dog.

"Ten dollars," the guy says.

"Ten dollars? This dog is amazing! Why on earth are you selling him so cheap?"

"Because he's a liar. He never did any of that shit."

NEVER TRUST AN ITALIAN

Angelo has broken his leg and his buddy Tony comes over to see him. Tony says, "How you doin?"

Angelo says, "Okay, but do me a favor goomba, run upstairs and get my slippers, me feet are freezing." Tony goes upstairs and sees Angelo's gorgeous 19-year old twin daughters lying on the bed.

He says, "Your dad sent me up here to have sex with both of you."

They say, "Prove it."

Tony shouts downstairs, "Hey Ange, both of 'em?"

Angelo shouts back, "Of course both of 'em, what good is fuckin' one?"

GREAT TRUTHS

"In my many years I have come to a conclusion that one useless man is a shame, two is a law firm and three or more is a congress."
– John Adams

"If you don't read the newspaper you are uninformed, if you do read the newspaper you are misinformed." – Mark Twain

"Suppose you were an idiot. And suppose you were a member of congress. But then I repeat myself." – Mark Twain

"I contend that for a nation to try to tax itself into prosperity is like a man standing in a bucket and trying to lift himself up by the handle." – Winston Churchill

"A government which robs Peter to pay Paul can always depend on the support of Paul." – George Bernard Shaw

"A liberal is someone who feels a great debt to his fellow man, which debt he proposes to pay off with your money."
– G. Gordon Liddy

"Democracy must be something more than two wolves and a sheep voting on what to have for dinner." – James Bovard, Civil Libertarian (1994)

"Foreign aid might be defined as a transfer of money from poor people in rich countries to rich people in poor countries." – Douglas Casey, Classmate of Bill Clinton at Georgetown University

"Giving money and power to government is like giving whiskey and car keys to teenage boys." – P.J. O'Rourke, Civil Libertarian

"Government's view of the economy could be summed up in a few short phrases: IF it moves, tax it. If it keeps moving, regulate it. And if it stops moving, subsidize it." – Ronald Reagan (1968)

"I don't make jokes. I just watch the government and report the facts." – Will Rogers

"If you think health care is expensive now, wait until you see what it costs when it's free!" -- P.J. O'Rourke

"In general, the art of government consists of taking as much money as possible from one party of the citizens to give to the other." – Voltaire (1764)

"Just because you do not take an interest in politics doesn't mean politics won't take an interest in you!" -- Pericles (circa 430 B.C.)

"No man's life, liberty, or property is safe while the legislature in session." – Mark Twain
"Talk is cheap…except when Congress does it."
– Anonymous.

"The government is like a baby's alimentary canal, with a happy appetite at one end and no responsibility at the other."
– Ronald Reagan

"The inherent vice of capitalism is the unequal sharing of the blessings. The inherent blessing of socialism is the equal sharing of misery." – Winston Churchill

"The only difference between a tax man and a taxidermist is that the taxidermist leaves the skin." -- Mark Twain

"The ultimate result of shielding men from the effects of folly is to fill the world with fools." – Herbert Spencer, English Philosopher (1820-1903)

"There is no distinctly Native American criminal class…save Congress. – Mark Twain

"What this country needs are more unemployed politicians."
– Edward Langley, Artist (1928-1995)

"A government big enough to give you everything you want, is strong enough to take everything you have"
– Thomas Jefferson

"We hang the petty thieves and appoint the great ones to public office." – Aesop

FIVE BEST SENTENCES

1. You cannot legislate the poor into prosperity, by legislating the wealth out of prosperity.

2. What one person receives without working for… another person must work for without receiving.

3. The government cannot give to anybody anything that the government does not first take from somebody else.

4. You cannot multiply wealth by dividing it.

5. When half of the people get the idea that they do not have to work, because the other half is going to take care of them, and when the other half gets the idea that it does no good to work, because somebody else is going to get what they work for, that is the beginning of the end of any nation!

THINGS YOU CAN ONLY SAY ON THANKSGIVING

1. Talk about a huge breast!
2. Tying the legs together keeps the inside moist.
3. It's Cool Whip time!
4. If I don't undo my pants, I'll burst!
5. That's one terrific spread.
6. I'm in the mood for a little dark meat.
7. Are you ready for seconds yet?
8. It's a little dry, do you still want to eat it?
9. Just wait your turn, you'll get some!
10. Don't play with your meat.
11. Just spread the legs open and stuff it in.
12. Do you think you'll be able to handle all these people at once?
13. I didn't expect everyone to come at once!
14. You still have a little bit on your chin.
15. How long will it take after you stick it in?
16. You'll know it's ready when it pops up.
17. Wow, I didn't think I could handle all of that!
18. That's the biggest one I've ever seen.

WONG MARRIES WONG

Su Wong marries Lee Wong.

The next year, the Wongs have a new baby. The nurse brings out a lovely, healthy, bouncy, but definitely a Caucasian, WHITE baby boy.

Congratulations, says the nursed to the new parents. Well Mr. Wong, what will you and Mrs. Wong name the baby?

The puzzled father looks at his new baby boy and says, "Well, to Wong's don't make a white, so I think we will name him…Sum Ting Wong.

FOR THOSE WHO THOUGHT
THEY KNEW EVERYTHING

- The liquid inside young coconuts can be used as a substitute for - Blood Plasma.

- No piece of paper can be folded in half more than seven (7) times. Oh go ahead ... I'll wait....

- Donkeys kill more people annually than plane crashes or shark attacks - so, watch your Ass.

- You burn more calories sleeping than you do watching television.

- Oak trees do not produce acorns until they are fifty (50) years of age or older.

- The first product to have a bar code was Wrigley's gum.

- The King of Hearts is the only king without a mustache.

- American Airlines saved $40,000 in 1987 by eliminating one (1) olive from each salad served in first-class.

- Venus is the only planet that rotates clockwise. (Since Venus is normally associated with women, what does this tell you?) (That women are going the 'right' direction...?)

- Apples, not caffeine, are more efficient at waking you up in the morning.

- Most dust particles in your house are made from DEAD SKIN!

- The first owner of the Marlboro Company died of lung cancer. So did the first Marlboro Man.

- Walt Disney was afraid of mice.

- Pearls melt in vinegar!

- The three most valuable brand names on earth: Marlboro, Coca Cola, and Budwiser, in that order.

- It is possible to lead a cow upstairs…but, not downstairs.

- A duck's quack doesn't echo, and no one knows why.

- Dentists have recommended that a toothbrush be kept at least six (6) feet away from a toilet to avoid airborne particles resulting from the flush. (I keep my toothbrush in the living room now!)

- Turtles can breathe through their butts. (I know some people like that, don't YOU?)

Now you know everything! Remember, knowledge is everything, so pass it on…. Watch out for Turtle Butts and go move your toothbrush!!

GOTTA PEE

Two women friends had gone for a girls' night out. Both are very faithful and loving wives, however they had gotten over-enthusiastic with the Bacarti Breezers.

Incredibly drunk and walking home they needed to pee, so they stopped in the cemetery.

One of them had nothing to wipe with so she thought she would take off her panties and use them.

Her friend however was wearing a rather expensive pair of panties and did not want to ruin them.

She was lucky enough to squat down next to a grave that had a wreath with a ribbon on it, so she proceeded to wipe with that.

After the girls did their business, they proceeded to go home.

The next day, the husband of one of the women was concerned that his normally sweet and innocent wife was still in bed hung over, so he phoned the other husband and said; "These girl nights have got to stop! I'm starting to suspect the worst. My wife came home with no panties!!

"That's nothing," said the other husband, "Mine came back with a card stuck to her ass that said, 'From all of us at the Fire Station. We'll never forget you.'"

"I'M 76 AND TIRED" BILL COSBY

I'M 76 - Except for a brief period in the 50's when I was doing my National Service, I've worked hard since I was 17. Except for some some serious health challenges, I put in 50-hour weeks, and didn't call in sick in nearly 40 years. I made a reasonable salary, but I didn't inherit my job or my income, and I worked to get where I am. Given the economy, it looks as though retirement was a bad idea, and I'm tired. Very tired.

I'M TIRED of being told that I have to "spread the wealthy" to people who don't have my work ethic. I'm tired of being told the government will take the money I earned, by force if necessary, and give it to people too lazy to earn it.

I'M TIRED of being told that Islam is a "Religion of Peace," when every day I can read dozens of stories of Muslim men killing their sisters, wives and daughters for their family "honor'; of Muslims rioting over some slight offense; of Muslims murdering Christian and Jews because they aren't "believers"; of Muslims burning schools for girls' of Muslims stoning teenage rape victims to death for "adultery"; of Muslims mutilating the genitals of little girls; all in the name of Allah, because the Qur'an and Shari's law tells them to.

I'M TIRED of being told that out of "tolerance for other cultures" we must let Saudi Arabia and other Arab countries use our oil money to fund mosques and madrassa Islamic schools to preach hate in Australia, New Zealand, UK, America and Canada, while no one from these countries are allowed to fund a church, synagogue or religious school in Saudi Arabia or any other Arab country to teach love and tolerance.

I'M TIRED of being told I must lower my living standard to fight global warming, which no one is allowed to debate.

I'M TIRED of being told that drug addicts have a disease, and I must help support and treat them, and pay for the damage they do. Did a giant germ rush out of the dark alley, grab them, and stuff white powder up their noses or stick a needle in their arm while they tried to fight it off?

I'M TIRED of hearing wealthy athletes, entertainers and politicians of all parties talking about innocent mistakes, stupid mistakes or youthful mistakes, when we all know they think their only mistake was getting caught. I'm tired of people with a sense of entitlement, rich or poor.

I'M REALLY TIRED of people who don't take responsibility for their lives and actions. I'm tired of hearing them blame the government, or discrimination or big-whatever for their problems.

I'M ALSO TIRED and fed up with seeing young men and women in their teens and early 20's be-deck them selves in tattoos and face studs, thereby making themselves um-employable and claiming money from the Government.

YES, I'M DAMN TIRED. But I'm also glad to be 76. Because, mostly, I'm not going to have to see the world these people are making. I'm just sorry for my granddaughter and her children. Thank God I'm on the way out and not on the way in.

MEN OVER SIXTY

Q - Where can men over the age of 60 find younger, sexy women who are interested?
A - Try a bookstore under fiction.

Q - What can a man do while his wife is going through menopause?
A - Keep busy. If you're handy with tools, you can finish the basement. When you're done you'll have a nice place to live.

Q - Someone has told me that menopause is mentioned in the bible.
A - Yes, Matthew 14:92 "And Mary rode Joseph's ass all the way to Egypt..."

Q - How can you increase the heart rate of your 60-plus year old husband?
A - Tell him you're pregnant.

Q - How can you avoid that terrible curse of the elderly wrinkles?
A - Take off your glasses.

Q - Seriously! What can I do for these Crow's feet and all those wrinkles on my face?
A - Go braless. It will usually pull them out.

Q - Why should 60-plus year old people use valet parking?
A - Valtes don't forget where they parked the car.

Q - Is it common for 60-year olds to have problems with short-term memory storage?
A - Storage memory is not a problem, retrieving it is the problem.

Q - As people age, do they sleep more soundly?
A - Yes, but usually in the afternoon.

Q - Where should 60-plus year olds look for eye glasses?
A - On their foreheads.

Q - What is the most common remark made by 60-plus year olds when they enter antique stores?
A - "Gosh, I remember these!"

OUR DAUGHTERS

We need to teach our DAUGHTERS the difference between a man who FLATTERS her and a man who COMPLEMENTS her.

A man who SPENDS MONY on her and a man who INVESTS in her.

A man who views her as PROPERTY and a man who views her PROPERLY.

A man who LUSTS after her and a man who LOVES her.

A man who believes HE is GOD'S GIFT to women and a man who remembers a WOMAN was GOD'S GIFT to MAN.

And then teach OUR SONS to be that kind of man!

POCKET TAZER STUN GUN,
A GREAT GIFT FOR THE WIFE

Last weekend I saw something at Larry's Pistol & Pawn Shop that sparked my interest. The occasion was our 15ᵗʰ anniversary and I was looking for a little something extra for my wife Julie. What I came across was a 100,000-volt, pocket/purse-size Tazer.

The effects of the Tazer were supposed to be short lived, with no long term adverse affect on your assailant, allowing her adequate time to retreat to safety....?

WAY TOO COOL! Long story short, I bought the device and brought it home...I loaded two AAA batteries in the darn thing and pushed the button. Nothing! I was disappointed. I learned, however, that if I pushed the button and pressed it against a metal surface at the same time, I'd get the blue arc of electricity darting back and forth between the prongs.

AWESOME!! Unfortunately, I have yet to explain to Julie what that burn spot is on the face of her microwave.

Okay, so I was home alone with this new toy, thinking to myself that it couldn't be all that bad with only two AAA batteries, right?

There I sat in my recliner, my cat Gracie looking on intently (trusting little soul) while I was reading the directions and thinking that I really needed to try this thing out on a flesh & blood moving target.

I must admit I thought about zapping Gracie (for a fraction of a second) and then thought better of it. She is such a sweet cat. But, if

I was going to give this thing to my wife to protect herself against a mugger, I did want some assurance that it would work as advertised.

Am I wrong?

So, there I sat in a pair of shorts and a tank top with my reading glasses perched delicately on the bridge of my nose, directions in one hand, and Tazer in the other.

The directions said that; a one-second burst would shock and disorient your assailant; a two-second
Burst was supposed to cause muscle spasms and a major loss of bodily control; and a three-second burst would reportedly make your assailant flop on the ground like a fish out of water. Any burst longer than three seconds would be wasting the batteries.

All the while I'm looking at this little device measuring about 5" long, less that ¾ inch in diameter (loaded with two itsy, bitsy AAA batteries): pretty cute really, and thinking to myself, 'no possible way!'

What happened next is almost beyond description, but I'll do my best.

I'm sitting there alone. Gracie, looking on with her head cocked to one side so as to say, 'Don't do it stupid,' reasoning that a one second burst from such a tiny lil ole thing couldn't hurt all that bad… I decided to give myself a one second burst just for the heck of it.

I touched the prongs to my naked thigh, pushed the button, and…

HOLY MOTHER OF GOD. WEAPONS OF MASS DESTRUCTION, WHAT THE!!!!!

I'm pretty sure Hulk Hogan ran in through the side door, picked me up in the recliner, then body slammed us both to the carpet, over and over and over again. I vaguely recall waking up on my side in the fetal position, with tears in my eyes, body soaking wet, both nipples on fire, testicles nowhere to be found, with my left arm tucked under my body in the oddest position, and tingling in my legs! The cat was making meowing sounds I had never heard before, clinging to a picture frame hanging above the fireplace, obviously in an attempt to avoid getting slammed by my body flopping all over the living room.

NOTE: If you ever feel compelled to 'mug yourself with a Tazer, one note of caution: There is NO such thing as a one-second burst when you zap yourself! You will not let go of that thing until it is dislocated from your hand by a violent thrashing about on the floor! A three-second burst would be considered conservative!

A minute or so later (I can't be sure, as time was a relative thing at that point), I collected my wits (what little I had left), sat up and surveyed the landscape.

My bent reading glasses were on the mantel of the fireplace. The recliner was upside down and about 8 feet or so from where is originally was. My triceps, right thigh and both nipples were still twitching. My face felt like it had been shot up with Novocain, and my bottom lip weighed 88 lbs. I had no control over the drooling.

Apparently I had crapped in my shorts, but was too numb to know for sure, and my sense of smell was gone.
I saw a faint smoke cloud above my head, which I believe came from my hair.

I'm still looking for my testicles and I'm offering a significant reward for their safe return!

P.S. - My wife can't stop laughing about my experience, loved the gift and now regularly threatens me with it!

If you think education is difficult, try being stupid!!!!

OLD AGE

Old age, I decided, is a gift. I am now probably for the first time in my life, the person I have always wanted to be. Oh, not my body! I sometime despair over my body – the cellulite, the wrinkles, the baggy eyes, the jiggly thighs, and the sagging butt. And often I am taken back by the old lady who lives in my mirror, but I don't agonize over those things for long.

I would never trade my amazing friends, my wonderful life, my loving family for less gray hair or a flatter belly. As I've aged, I've become more kind to myself, and less critical of myself. I've become my own friend. I don't chide myself for eating that extra cookie, or for not making my bed, or for buying that silly cement gecko that I didn't need, but looks so ridiculous on my patio. I am entitled to overeat, to be messy, to be extravagant. I have seen too many dear friends leave this world too soon; before they understood the great freedom that comes with aging.

Whose business is it if I choose to read until 4:00 am, and sleep until noon? I will dance with myself to those wonderful tunes of the 50's and 60's, and if I at the same time wish to weep over a lost love, I will. I will walk the beach in a swim suit that is stretched over a bulging midriff, and will dive into the waves with abandon if I choose to, despite the pitying glances from the bikini set. They too, will get old.

I know I am sometimes forgetful. But there again, some of life is just as well forgotten – and I eventually remember the important things. Sure, over the years my heart has been broken. How can your heart not break when you lose a loved one, or a child suffers, or even when a beloved pet gets hit by a car? But broken hearts are what give us strength and understanding and compassion. A heart never broken is pristine and sterile and will never know the joy of being imperfect.

I am so blessed to have lived long enough to have my hair turn gray, and to have my youthful laughs be forever etched into deep groves on my face. So many have never laughed, and so many have died before their hair could turn silver.

I can say "no", and mean it. I can say "yes", and mean it. As you get older, it is easier to be positive. You care less about what other people think. I don't question myself anymore. I've even earned the right to be wrong.

I like being old. It has set me free. I like the person I have become. I am not going to live forever, but while I am still here, I will not waste time lamenting what could have been, or worrying about what will be. For the first time in my life, I don't have to have a reason to do the things I want to do. And I shall eat dessert every single day.

THE GRAY-HAIRED BRIGADE

They like to refer to us as senior citizens, old fogies, geezers, and in some cased dinosaurs. Some of us are "baby boomers" getting ready to retire. Others have been retired for some time.

We walk a little slower these days and our eyes and hearing are not what they once were. We have worked hard, raised our children, worshipped our God and grown old together. Yes, we are the ones some refer to as being over the hill and that is probably true. But before writing us off completely, there are a few things that need to be taken into consideration. In school we studied English, history, math, and science which enabled us to lead America into the technology age.

Most of us remember what outhouses were, many of us with firsthand experience. We remember the days of telephone party lines, 25 cent gasoline, and milk and ice being delivered to our homes. For those of you who don't know what an icebox is, today they are electric and referred to as refrigerators. A few even remember when cars were started with a crank. Yes, we lived those days. We are probably considered old fashioned and out-dated by many.

But there are a few things you need to remember before completely writing us off. We won World War II and fought in Korea and Vietnam. We can quote the pledge of allegiance, and know where to place our hand while doing so. We wore the uniform of our country with pride and lost many friends on the battlefield. We didn't fight for the Socialist States of America, we fought for the "Land of the Free and the Home of the Brave". We wore different uniforms, but carried the same flag. We know the words to the 'Star Spangled

Banner', and 'America the Beautiful' by heart, and you may even see some tears running down our cheeks as we sing.

We have lived what many of you have only read about in history books and we feel no obligation to apologize to anyone for America. Yes, we are old and slow these days but rest assured, we have at least one good fight left in us. We have loved this country, fought for it, and many died for it, now we are going to save it. It is our country and nobody is going to take it away from us.

We took oaths to defend America against all enemies, foreign and domestic, and that is an oath we plan to keep. There is no statute of limitation on the oath we took. There are those who want to destroy this land we love, but, like our founders, there is no way we are going to remain silent.

So the next time you have the chance to say the Pledge of Allegiance, stand up, put your hand over your heart, honor our country, and the next time you honor our Nation by the singing of our National Anthem, gentlemen, please remove your hats, and afterwards, thank God for the old geezers of the "Gray-Haired Brigade."

A COWBOY NAMED BUD

A cowboy named Bud was overseeing his herd in a remote mountainous pasture in Montana when suddenly a brand-new BMW advanced toward him out of a cloud of dust.

The driver, a young man in a Brioni suit, Gucci shoes, RayBan sunglasses and YSL tie, leaned out the window and asked the cowboy, "If I tell you exactly how many cows and calves you have in your herd, will you give me a calf?"

Bud looks at the man, who obviously is a yuppie, then looks at his peacefully grazing herd and calmly answers, "Sure, why not?"

The yuppie parks his car, whips out his Dell Notebook computer, connects it to his Cingular RAZR V3 cell phone, and surfs to a NASA page on the Internet, where he calls up a GPS satellite to get an exact fix on his location, which he then feeds to another NASA satellite that scans the area in an ultra-high-resolution photo.

The young man then opens the digital photo in Adobe Photoshop and exports it to an image processing facility in Hamburg, Germany…

Within seconds, he received an email on his Palm Pilot that the image has been processed and the data stored. He then accesses an MS-SQL database through an ODBC connected Excel spreadsheet with email on his Blackberry and, after a few minutes, receives a response.

Finally, he prints out a full-color, 150-page report on his hi-tech, miniaturized HP Laser Jet printer, turns to the cowboy and says, "You have exactly 1,586 cows and calves."

"That's right. Well, I guess you can take one of my calves." Says Bud.

He watches the young man select one of the animals and looks on with amusement as the young man stuffs it into the trunk of his car.

Then Bud says to the young man, "Hey, if I can tell you exactly what your business is, will you give me back my calf?"

The young man thinks about it for a second and then says, "Okay, why not?"

"You're a Congressman for the U.S. Government", says Bud.

"Wow! That's correct," says the yuppie, 'but how did you guess that?"

"No guessing required." answered the cowboy. "You showed up here even though nobody called you; you want to get paid for an answer I already knew, to a question I never asked. You used millions of dollars worth of equipment trying to show me how much smarter than me you are; and you don't know a thing about how working people make a living – or about cows, for that matter. This is a heard of sheep.

"Now give me back my dog."

LIFE IN CINCY

You know you live (or have lived) in/around Cincinnati if…

- You know the first pro baseball team ever was the Cincinnati Red Stockings. (1869)
- You remember watching Bob Shreve's "All night Theater."
- You call it 'pop' not a soda or a soft drink.
- You or your kids played KNOTHOLE ball not Little League.
- You know that Millcreek would not be a good name for bottled water.
- One of your favorite candies is a French Chew.
- You remember that Ruth Lyons put flowers around her microphone.
- You know that Norwood, Ohio is the only city that is completely surrounded by another city.
- You could take a picnic basket to Coney Island leave it on a table and it was still there at lunch time.
- You asked for a beer and it was brewed in Cincinnati.
- Before Wal-Mart there were Rink's, Ontario's, Zayer's and China Town.
- You know 'Paul Baby's" last name was Dixon.
- You watched "Hattie the Witch" featuring Larry Smith and his Puppets every afternoon.
- You remember Bob Shreve was on Channel 9 for the afternoon cartoon show.

- You remember the "Wild Mouse" and "Wild Cat" at Coney Island.

- For you more mature folks…you cruised up the Ohio River on the Island Queen to Coney Island and danced in Moonlight gardens and swam in Sunlight Pool.

- Christmas wasn't complete until you went downtown to the CG&E Building and saw the model trains.

- You were told by older relatives that Cincinnati was the first in the country to have a full time paid Fire Department back in 1853.

- We don't say, y'all, we say 'you guys' and that includes the women too and some say 'yous guys'.

- You know that Kahn's is "the wiener the world awaited."

- You know who said "This is the old left-hander rounding third and headed for home" on the Reds Broadcast (Joe Nuxhall, still the youngest MLB player at age 15).

- And you know who said "and this one belongs to the Reds" (Marty Brenneman).

- You remember that the Reds played at Crosley Field and then Riverfront Stadium.

- You remember the 'Streitman Biscuit Company' before it became Keeblers.

- You remember "Midwestern Hayride" and know who Kenny Price was.

- You shopped downtown at Shillitos, Pogues and McAlpins and for special things Mabley & Crew.

- You know who the Cool Ghoul was and what channel he was on (WXIX Channel 19).

- You knew who Bob Braun was before he sold furniture on late nite TV.

- You can sing the "Audience Wave" jingle from the 50-50 Club.

- You immediately recognize the name "Brent Spence" but don't know who he was (long time Democratic Congressman from Newport, KY).

- You know Ezzard Charles was Cincinnati's only Heavyweight Boxing Champion.

- You know that pigs do fly in Cincinnati, as can be seen by the four majestic winged pigs on the river front.

- You know that the Cincinnati Airport is not even in Ohio and that the letters CVG stand for Covington, KY.

- You know that 'Reading Road' is pronounced "RED'ing Road…not "REEDing Road".

- You know what bread is "Hearth-baked on Stone" (Rubels' Rye Bread).

- You remember when the first "Gold Star Chili" parlor was named "Hamburger Heaven" and was in Mr. Washington just across from the old movie theater.

- You know who said) and you were very annoyed by), "I don't care about making money…I just love to sell carpet.

- You spend every weekend in October going to a different "Oktoberfest."

- You remember when the Bengals last went to the Super Bowl, and gas was $1.09 a gallon.

- You have friends and neighbors with names like Gukenberger, Hirlinger, Schottlekotte, Schraffenberger and Schoenling.

- You know who Al Schottelkotte was.

- You know exactly when each parish has its festival and which ones are the best.

- You think that the only 'tri-state' area in the US is Ohio, Kentucky and Indiana (some say that is how Okeana got its name...but those who live there know it was named after a local Native American Princess.)

- During a taste test you can tell the difference in the following chili's: Skyline, Cincinnati Recipe, Empress, Gold Star, Camp Washington (pronounced WARSHington), Worthmore and Dixie.

- And you know that chili is served in Chili Parlors, not restaurants.

- You know how to spell Cincinnati and it is not: Cincinti, Cincinatti, Cincinnatti, Cinnanatti.

- And you know it is pronounced "sin-sin-nat-tee" not "sin-sin-nat-ta."

- You "warsh" your clothes.

- You go to "Cook-outs" not BBQ's.

- You wear "gym shoes" not sneakers or tennis shoes.

- Anytime anyone wants to know where you graduated from, you answer without hesitation, your high school...no one cares where you went to college.

- One of the best summer treats, a Black Cow using Barq's Root Beer or a Red Cow, using Barq's Cream Soda.

- You know how to "Save Cash with Cash."

- You know the "Cross Town Shootout" is not a wild west gun fight, but the most important college basketball game during the season, between XU and UC.

- You take a leisurely summer drive through a suburban neighborhood and you see a cornhole game on every block.

- You know the Daniel Carter Beard Bridge is called the Big Mac Bridge.

- You know it is not Easter without Papas Cream Eggs.

- Instead of saying "what?" you say "please?"

- You add an 's' to the end of grocery store names, such as Kroger(s), and Meijer(s).

- You drive on roads that change names at the county line, such as Loveland-Maderia, Fields-Ertel, Hamilton-Mason and Cincinnati-Dayton.

- You can buy beer by driving through a drive thru pole barn, or at the "Pony Keg".

- You recognize Anthony Munoz as a former NFL player not a furniture salesman.

- You remind people that Pompillios was in the movie Rainman.

- You understand that traffic reports which ignore road names and use locations such as: "Cut in the hill', The Lockland Split, Five Mile, Wards Corner, Kenwood "Cut in the Hill', and The "S" curve.

- You know that Roy Rogers, Doris Day, "Bootsy" Collins and Nick Lachey are famous entertainers that came from Cincinnati and Peter Frampton is a well known musician that is a 'naturalized" Cincinnatian.

- Your local convenience store sounds like a labor union: United Dairy Farmers.

- You believe that Pete Rose should be in the hall of fame.

- You miss Marge Schott and Schottzie.

- You know that everyone has an "Uncle Al."

- Your favorite "Coney Island" isn't in New York.

- You know what brats and metts are.

- You have goetta and eggs for breakfast.

- You know who Skipper Ryle was.

- You are at a Bob Evans Restaurant and don't think it is strange to see someone put ketchup on their eggs.

- You like Nick Clooney better than George Clooney.

- You know how Jerry Springer got his start (and that you shouldn't write a check to a prostitute.)

- You think a mixed marriage is where an East-Sider marries a West-Sider.

- You know what "cream ale" is, and you think that all cream soda should be bright red.

- You can visit Lebanon, California, Moscow, Wyoming and go "Over the Rhine" all in the same day.

- You know what is at "Where Paddock meets Vine at the Big Indian Sign" – at least if you're ever been to the east side.

ESPECIALLY DOGS

- A life without a dog is a mistake. —Carl Zuchmayer

- Women and cats will do what pleases them, dogs and men should relax and get used to the idea. —Robert A. Heinlein

- The love for animals embraces the culture level of the people. —F. Salvoches

- When you leave a dog behind because he "grew old", your children will learn the lesson. Maybe they will do the same to you when you are an old man. Think about it!

- Love is when your dog licks your face, even if you leave it alone the whole day. Anita, 4 years old

- It doesn't matter if an animal can reason. It matters only that it is capable of suffering and that is why I consider it my neighbor. —Albert Schweitzer

- We can judge the heart of a man according to his love for animals. —Immanuel Kant

- "Don't call me dog. I do not deserve such a high qualification…I am not as faithful or loyal….I am only a human being".

- "Every child should have two things; a dog, and a mother who let him have one."

- Do not accept the admiration of your dog as an obvious conclusion that you are wonderful. —Ann Landers

- "The dog knows, but does not know that he knows'.   —Pierre Teilhard de Chardin

- Who said you can not buy happiness, when you are thinking about puppies". —Gene Hill

- "If your dog doesn't like someone, you probably should not either".

- A dog is the only thing on earth that will love you more than you will love yourself. —Jack Billings

- You can live without a dog, but it is not worthwhile.

- If a dog does not come to you after looking you in the face, it is better that you go home and examine your conscience. —Woodrow Wilson

- Buying a dog may be the only opportunity that a human being has to choose a relative.

- —Mordecai Siega

- You can say any foolish thing to a dog and the dog will look at you in a way that seems to say: "My God, he is right! That would not have occurred to me."

- —Dave Berry

- Setting back in the evening, stargazing and stroking your dog, is an infallible remedy. —Ralph Waldo Emerson

- There is no better psychiatrist in the world than a puppy licking your face. —Woodrow Wilson

- Somewhere in the rain, there will always be an abandoned dog that prevents you from being happy.   —Aldus Huxley

- The greatness of a nation and its moral progress can be judged by the manner in which its animals are treated. —Mahatma Gandhi

- Many, who have dedicated their life to love, can tell us less about this subject than a child who lost his dog yesterday. — Thornton Wilder

- Dogs are not everything in life, but they make it complete. —Roger Caras

- Just thinking that my dog loves me more than I love him, I feel ashamed. —Konrad Loring

- "They will be our friends forever, always and always."

ASSAILANT SUFFERS INJURIES FROM FALL

Orville Smith, a store manager for Best Buy in Augusta, GA., told police he observed a male customer, later identified as Tyrone Jackson of Augusta, on surveillance cameras putting a laptop computer under his jacket. When confronted the man became irate, knocked down an employee, drew a knife and ran for the door.

Outside on the sidewalk were four Marines collecting toys for the Tots program. Smith said the Marines stopped the man, but he stabbed one of the marines, Cpl. Phillip Duggan, in the back; the injury did not appear to be severe.

After Police and an ambulance arrived at the scene Cpl. Dugan was transported for treatment.

"The subject was also transported to the local hospital with two broken arms, a broken ankle, a broken leg, several missing teeth, possible broken ribs, multiple contusions, assorted lacerations, a broken nose and a broken jaw...injuries he sustained when he slipped and fell off the curb after stabbing the Marine," according to a police report.

CAPTAIN FRANCESCO SCHETTINO SUBSCRIBED TO THIS THEORY

The current plight of the Costa Concordia reminds me of a comment made by Winston Churchill.

After his retirement he was cruising the Mediterranean on an Italian cruise liner and some Italian journalist asked why an ex British Prime Minister should chose an Italian ship.

There are three things I like about being on an Italian cruise ship said Churchill.

First their cuisine in unsurpassed. Second their service is superb. And then, in time of emergency, there is none of this nonsense about women and children first.

2012

DAVID FEHERTY QUOTES
(PGA GOLD ANNOUNCER)

- "Fortunately, he (Rory) is 22 years old, so his right wrist should be the strongest muscle in his body."

- "That ball is so far left, Lassie couldn't find it if it was wrapped in bacon."

- "I am sorry Nick Faldo couldn't be here this week. He is attending the birth of his next wife."

- Tommy Gainey's grip – "They look like two lobsters trying to mate."

- "They don't do comedy at the Masters. The Masters, for me, is like holding onto the really big collection of gas for a week. It's like having my buttocks surgically clenched at Augusta General Hospital on Wednesday, and surgically unclenched on Monday on the way to Hilton Head."

- Jim Furyk's swing - "It looks like an octopus falling out of a tree."

- "He's (Luke Donald) a bloody walking ATM. I slid my AmEx between the cheeks of his ass and out popped $500."

- Describing VJ's prodigious practice regime - "VJ hits more balls than Elton John's chin."

- "That's a great shot with that swing."

- "It's OK - the bunker stopped it."

- At Augusta 2011 - "It's just a glorious day. The only way to ruin a day like this would be to play golf on it."

- "That was a great shot – if they'd put the pin there today."

- "All you need for a happy life is good health and a bad memory."

- "Everything moves except his bowels."

- "Watching Phil Mickelson play golf is like watching a drunk chasing a balloon near the edge of a cliff."

WITH EURO GOING DOWN,
FORD TO ACQUIRE RENAULT

Ford has announced plans to acquire French automaker Renault and engineering teams have already joined forces to create the perfect small car for women.

Mixing the Renault "Clio" and the Ford "Taurus", they have designed a "Clitaurus". It comes in pink and the average male care thief won't be able to find it, let alone turn it on, even if someone tells him where it is and how to do it.

Rumor has it though, that it leaks transmission fluid once a month and can be a real bitch to start in the morning! Some have reported that on cold winter mornings, when you really need it, you can't get it to turn over.

New models are initially fun to own, but very costly to maintain and horribly expensive to get rid of. Used models may initially appear to have curb appeal and a low price, but eventually have an increased appetite for fuel, and the curb weight typically increases with age. Manufacturers are baffled as to how the size of the trunk increases, but say that the paint may just make it LOOK bigger.

This model is not expected to reach collector status. Most owners find it is best to lease one, and replace it as needed.

HELLO HANDSOME, MY NAME IS ROSE

The first day of school our professor introduced himself and challenged us to get to know someone we didn't already know. I stood up to look around when a gentle hand touched my shoulder.

I turned around to find a wrinkled, little old lady beaming up at me with a smile that lit up her entire being.

She said, "Hi handsome, my name is Rose. I'm eighty-seven years old. Can I give you a hug?"

I laughed and enthusiastically responded, "Of course you may" and she gave me a giant squeeze.

"Why are you in college at such a young, innocent age?" I asked.

She jokingly replied, "I'm here to meet a rich man, get married, and have a couple of kids…." "No seriously," I asked. I was curious what may have motivated her to be taking on this challenge at her age.
"I always dreamed of having a college education and now I'm getting one!" She told me.

After class we walked to the student union building and shared a chocolate milkshake.

We became instant friends. Every day for the next three months we would leave class together and talk nonstop. I was always mesmerized listening to this "time machine" as she shared her wisdom and experience with me.

Over the course of the year, Rose became a campus icon and she easily made friends wherever she went. She loved to dress up and she reveled in the attention bestowed upon her from the other students. She was living it up.

At the end of the semester we invited Rose to speak at our football banquet. I'll never forget what she taught us. She was introduced and stepped up to the podium. As she began to deliver her prepared speech, she dropped her three by five cards on the floor.

Frustrated and a little embarrassed she leaned into the microphone and simply said, "I'm sorry I'm so jittery. I gave up beer for Lent and this whisky is killing me! I'll never get my speech back in order so let me just tell you what I know."

As we laughed she cleared her throat and began, "We do not stop playing because we are old; we grow old because we stop playing. There are only four secrets to staying young, being happy and achieving success. You have to laugh and find humor every day. You've got to have a dream. When you lose your dreams, you die. We have so many people walking around who are dead and don't know it! There is a huge difference between growing older and growing up.

If you are nineteen years old and lie in bed for one full year and don't do one productive thing, you will turn twenty years old. If I am eighty-seven years old and stay in bed for a year and never do anything, I will turn eighty-eight.

Anybody can grow older. That doesn't take any talent or ability. The idea is to grow up by always finding opportunity in change. Have no regrets.

The elderly usually don't have regrets for what we did, but rather for things we did not do. The only people who fear death are those with regrets."

She concluded her speech by courageously singing "The Rose."

She challenged each of us to study the lyrics and live them out in our daily lives. At the year's end Rose finished the college degree she had begun all those months ago.

One week after graduation Rose died peacefully in her sleep.

Over two thousand college students attended her funeral in tribute to the wonderful woman who taught by example that it's never too late to be all you can possibly be.

Remember, growing older is mandatory. Growing up is optional. We make a living by what we get. We make a life by what we give.

THE BLACK BRA (AS TOLD BY A WOMAN)

I had lunch with 2 of my unmarried friends. One is engaged, one is a mistress, and I have been married for 20+ years.

We were chatting about our relationships and decided to amaze our men by greeting them at the door wearing a black bra, stiletto heels and a mask over our eyes. We agreed to meet in a few days to exchange notes. Here's how it went.

My engaged friend: The other night when my boyfriend came over he found me with a black leather bodice, tall stilettos and a mask. He saw me and said, "You are the woman of my dreams. I love you." Then we made passionate love all night long.

The mistress: Me too! The other night I met my lover at his office and I was wearing a Raincoat, under it the black bra, heels and mask over my eyes. When I opened the raincoat he didn't say a word, but he started to tremble and we had wild sex all night.

Then I had to share my story: When my husband came home I was wearing the black bra, black stockings, stilettos and a mask over my eyes. When he came in the door and saw me and said, "What's for dinner, Batman?"

ABBOT & COSTELLO ON UNEMPLOYMENT

Costello: I want to talk about the unemployment rate in America.

Abbott: Good subject. Terrible times. It's 9%.

Costello: That many people are out of work?

Abbott: No, that's 16%.

Costello: You just said 9%.

Abbott: 9% unemployed.

Costello: Right 9% out of work.

Abbott: No, that's 16%.

Costello: Okay, so it's 16% unemployed.

Abbott: No, that's 9%...

Costello: Wait a minute. Is it 9% or 16%?

Abbott: 9% are unemployed. 16% are out of work.

Costello: If you are out of work you are unemployed.

Abbott: No, you can't count the "Out of Work" as the unemployed. You have to look for work to be unemployed.

Costello: But, they are out of work!!!

Abbott: No, you miss my point.

Costello: What point?

Abbott: Someone who doesn't look for work, can't be counted with those who look for work. It wouldn't be fair.

Costello: To who?

Abbott: The unemployed.

Costello: But they are ALL out of work.

Abbott:	No, the unemployed are actively looking for work... Those who are out of work stopped looking. They gave up. And, if you give up, you are no longer in the ranks of unemployed.
Costello:	So if you're off the unemployment rolls, that would count as less unemployed?
Abbott:	Unemployment would go down. Absolutely!
Costello:	The unemployment just goes down because you don't look for work?
Abbott:	Absolutely it goes down. That's how you get to 9%. Otherwise it would be 16%. You don't want to read about 16% unemployment, do ya?
Costello:	That would be frightening.
Abbott:	Absolutely.
Costello:	Wait, I got a question for you. That means they're two ways to bring down the unemployment number?
Abbott:	Two ways is correct.
Costello:	And unemployment can also go down if you stop looking for a job?
Abbott:	Correct.
Costello:	And unemployment can also go down if someone gets a job.
Abbott:	Bingo!
Costello:	So there are two ways to bring unemployment down, and the easier of the two is to just stop looking for work.
Abbott:	Now you're thinking like an economist.
Costello:	I don't even know what the hell I just said!

GARFIELD ON THE OIL CRISIS

A lot of folks can't understand how we came to have an oil shortage her in our country.

Well, there's a very simple answer.

Nobody bothered to check the oil. We just didn't know we were getting low. The reason for that is purely geographical.

Our oil is located in: Alaska, California, Coastal Florida, Coastal Louisiana, Coastal Alabama, Coastal Mississippi, Coastal Texas, North Dakota, Wyoming, Colorado, Kansas, Oklahoma, Pennsylvania, and Texas.

Our dip sticks are located in DC.

Any questions? No? Didn't think so.

UPS PILOT MAINTENANCE

Remember it takes a college degree to fly a plane, but only a high school diploma to fix one; a reassurance to those of us who fly routinely in our jobs.

After every flight UPS pilots fill out a form, called a 'gripe sheet,' which tells mechanics about problems with the aircraft. The mechanics correct the problems; document their repairs on the form, and then pilots review the gripe sheets before the next flight.

Never let it be said that ground crews lack a sense of humor. Here are some actual maintenance complaints submitted by UPS pilots (marked with a P) and the solutions recorded (marked with a S) by maintenance engineers.

By the way, UPS is the only major airline that has never, ever, had an accident.

P: Left inside main tire almost needs replacement.
S: Almost replaced left inside main tire.

P: Test flight OK, except auto-land very rough.
S: Auto-land not installed on this aircraft.

P: Something loose in cockpit.
S: Something tightened in cockpit.

P: Dead bugs on windshield.
S: Live bugs on back-order.

P: Autopilot in altitude-hold mode produces a 200-feet-per-minute descent.
S: Cannot reproduce problem on ground.

P: Evidence of leak on right main landing gear.
S: Evidence removed.

P: DME volume unbelievably loud.
S: DME volume set to more believable level.

P: Friction locks cause throttle levers to stick.
S: That's what friction locks are for.

P: IFF inoperative in OFF mode.
S: IFF is always inoperative in OFF mode.

P: Suspected crack in windshield.
S: Suspect you're right.

P: Number 3 engine missing.
S: Engine found on right wing after brief search.

P: Aircraft handles funny.
S: Aircraft warned to straighten up, fly right and be serious.

P: target radar hums.
S: Reprogramming target radar with lyrics.

P: Mouse in cockpit.
S: Cat installed.

P: Noise coming from under instrument panel. Sounds like a midget pounding on something with a hammer.

S: Took hammer away from the midget.

SOUTHERN INGENUITY

One morning three South Carolina good old boys and three Yankees were in a ticket line at the Spartanburg train station heading to Columbia for a big football game.

The three Northerners each brought a ticket and watched as the three Southern bought just one ticket among them.

"How are the three of you going to travel on one ticket"? asked one of the Yankees.

"Watch and learn" answered one of the boys from the south.

When the six travelers boarded the train, the three Yankees sat down, but the 3 Southerners crammed into a bathroom together and closed the door.

Shortly after the train departed, the conductor came around to collect tickets.

He knocked on the bathroom door and said, "Tickets please." The door opened just a crack and a single arm emerged with a ticket in hand. The Conductor took it and moved on.

The Yankees saw this happen and agreed it was quite a clever idea. Indeed, so clever that they decided to do the same thing on the return trip and save some money.

That evening after the game when they got to the Columbia train station, they bought a single ticket for the return trip while to their astonishment the three Southerners didn't buy even one ticket.

"How are you going to travel without a ticket?" asked one of the perplexed Yankees.

"Watch and learn", answered one of the Southern boys.

When they boarded the train the three Northerners crammed themselves into a bathroom and the three Southerners crammed themselves into the other bathroom across from it.

Shortly after the train began to move, one of the Southerners left their bathroom and walked quietly over to the Yankee's bathroom. He knocked on the door and said "ticket please".

There's just no way on God's green earth to explain how the Yankees won the war...

PORCUPINE

Fable of the Porcupine

It was the coldest winter ever. Many animals died because of the cold.

The porcupines, realizing the situation, decided to group together to keep warm. This way they covered and protected themselves; but the quills of each one wounded their closest companions.

After awhile, they decided to distance themselves on from the other and they began to die, alone and frozen. So they had to make a choice; either accept the quills of their companions or disappear from the Earth. Wisely, they decided to go back to being together. They learned to live with the little wounds caused by the close relationship with their companions in order to receive the heat that came from the others. This wan they were able to survive.

The best relationships are not the one that brings together perfect people, but when each individual learn to live with the imperfections of others and can admire the other person's good qualities.

The moral of the story is: Just learn to live with all the Pricks in your life!

HUSBAND DAY CARE CENTER

Located near our office, we have a Saloon and Eatery with this sign posted in the window.

HUSBAND Day Care Center.
Need time to relax?
Need time to yourself?
Want to go shopping?
Leave your husband with us!
We'll look after him for you!
You only pay for his food and drinks!

SCIENCE PUNS

Scientific Conversions:

Ratio of an igloo's circumference to its diameter = Eskimo Pi.
2000 pounds of Chinese soup = Won Ton

1 millionth of a mouthwash = 1 microscope

Time between slipping on a peel and smacking the pavement = 1 bananosecond

Weight an evangelist carries with God = 1 milligram

Time it takes to sail 220 yards at 1 nautical mile per hour = Knotfurlong

16.5 feet in the Twilight Zone = 1 Rod Serling

Half of a large intestine = semicolon1,000,000 aches = 1 megahertz

Basic unit of laryngitis = 1 horsepower

Shortest distance between two jokes = A straight line

453.6 graham crackers = 1 pound cake

1 million-million microphones = 1 megaphone

2 million bicycles = 2 megacycles

365.25 days = 1 unicycle

2000 mockingbirds = 1 kilomockingbirds

52 cards = 1 decacards

1 kilogram of falling figs = 1 Fig Newton

1000 milliliters of wet socks = 1 literhosen

1 millionth of a fish = 1 microfiche

1 trillion pins = 1 terrapin

10 rations = 1 decoration

100 rations = 1 C-ration

4 nickels = 2 paradigms

2.4 statute miles of intravenous surgical tubing at Yale University Hospital = 1 IV League

100 Senators = Not 1 decision

TECH SUPPORT

Tech:	What kind of computer do you have?
Customer:	A white one.
Tech:	Click on the 'my computer' icon on the left of the screen.
Customer:	Your left or my left?
Customer:	Hi, good afternoon, this is Martha, I can't print. Every time I try, it says, 'Can't find printer.' I've even lifted the printer and placed it in front of the monitor, but the computer still says he can't find it.
Tech:	What's on your monitor now, ma'am?
Customer:	A teddy bear my boyfriend bought for me at the 7-11.
Customer:	My keyboard is not working anymore.
Tech:	Are you sure it's plugged into the computer?
Customer:	No, I can't get behind the computer.
Tech:	Pick up your keyboard and walk 10 paces back.
Customer:	OK!
Tech:	Did the keyboard come with you?
Customer:	Yes.
Tech:	That means the keyboard is not plugged in.
Customer:	I can't get on the Internet.
Tech:	Are you sure you used the right password?
Customer:	Yes, I'm sure. I saw my colleague do it.
Tech:	Can you tell me what the password was?
Customer:	Five dots.

Tech:	What anti-virus program do you use?
Customer:	Netscape.
Tech:	That's not an anti-virus program.
Customer:	Oh, sorry…Internet Explorer…

Customer: I have a huge problem. A friend has placed a screen saver on my computer, but every time I move the mouse, it disappears.

Tech:	How may I help you?
Customer:	I'm writing my first email.
Tech:	OK, and what seems to be the problem?
Customer:	Well, I have the letter 'a' in the address, but how do I get the little circle around it?

Tech: Are you running it under windows?
Customer: No, my desk is next to the door, but that is a good point. The man sitting in the cubicle next to me is under a window, and his printer is working fine.

Tech: Okay, Bob. Let's press the control and escape keys at the same time. That brings up a task list in the middle of the screen. Now type the letter 'P' to bring up the Program Manager.
Customer: I don't have a P.
Tech: On your keyboard, Bob.
Customer: What do you mean?
Tech: 'P'…. on your keyboard, Bob.
Customer: I'M NOT GOING TO DO THAT!

Anger is a feeling that makes your mouth work faster than your MIND!

LEE TREVINO ... TRUE STORY AS TOLD BY HIM

One day, shortly after joining the PGA tour in 1965, Lee Trevino, a professional golfer and married man, was at his home in Dallas, Texas mowing his front lawn, as he always did.

A lady driving by in a big, shiny Cadillac stopped in front of his house, lowered the window and asked, "Excuse me, do you speak English?" Lee responded, "Yes Ma'am, I do."

The lady then asked: "What do you charge to do yard work?" Lee said, "Well, the lady in this house lets me sleep with her."

The lady hurriedly put the car into gear and sped off.

AIRLINE CAPTAIN

Letter from an airline pilot:

He writes: My lead flight attendant came to me and said, "We have an H.R. on this flight." (H.R. stands for human remains.) "Are they military?" I asked.

"Yes" she said. "Is there an escort/" I asked. "Yes, I've already assigned him a seat". "Would you please tell him to come to the flight deck? You can board him early." I said.

A short while later, a young army sergeant entered the flight deck. He was the image of the perfectly dressed soldier. He introduced himself and I asked him about his soldier. The escort of these fallen soldiers talks about them as if they are still alive and still with us.

"My soldier is on his way back to Virginia," he said. He proceeded to answer my questions, but offered no words. I asked him if there was anything I could do for him and he said no. I told him that he had the toughest job in the military and that I appreciated the work that he does for the families of our fallen soldiers. The first officer and I got up out of our seats to shake his hand. He left the flight deck to find his seat.

We completed our pre-flight checks, pushed back and performed an uneventful departure. About 30 minutes into our flight I received a call from the lead flight attendant in the cabin. "I just found out the family of the soldier we are carrying, is on board", she said. She then proceeded to tell me that the father, mother, wife and 2-year old daughter were escorting their son, husband, and father home. The family was upset because they were unable to see the container that the soldier was in before we left. We were on our way to a major hub at which the family was going to wait for hours for the connecting flight home to Virginia.

The father of the soldier told the flight attendant that knowing his son was below him in the cargo compartment and being unable to see him was too much for him and the family to bear. He had asked the flight attendant if there was anything that could be done to allow them to see him upon our arrival. The family wanted to be outside by the cargo door to watch the soldier being taken off the airplane. I could hear the desperation in the flight attendants voice when she asked me if there was anything I could do. "I'm on it", I said. I told her that I would get back to her.

Airborne communication with my company normally occurs in the form of e-mail like messages. I decided to bypass this system and contact my flight dispatcher directly on a secondary radio. There is a radio operator in the operations control center who connects you to the telephone of the dispatcher. I was in direct contact with the dispatcher. I explained the situation I had on board with the family and what it was the family wanted. He said he understood and that he would get back with me.

Two hours went by and I had not heard from the dispatcher. We were going to get busy soon and I needed to know what to tell the family. I sent a text message asking for an update. I saved the return message from the dispatcher and the following is the text:

"Captain, sorry it has taken so long to get back with you. There is policy on this now and I had to check on a few things. Upon your arrival a dedicated escort team will meet the aircraft. The team will escort the family to the ramp and plane side. A van will be used to load the remains with a secondary van for the family. The family will be taken to their departure area and escorted into the terminal where the remains can be seen on the ramp. It is a private area for the family only. When the connecting aircraft arrives, the family will be escorted onto the ramp and plane side to watch the remains being loaded for the final leg home. Captains, most of us here in flight control are veterans. Please pass our condolences on to the family, Thanks."

I sent a message back telling flight control thanks for a good job. I printed out the message and gave it to the lead flight attendant to pass on to the father. The lead flight attendant was very thankful and told me, "You have no idea how much this will mean to them."

Things started getting busy for the descent, approach and landing. After landing, we cleared the runway ant taxied to the ramp area. The ramp is huge with 15 gates on either side of the alleyway. It is always a busy area with aircraft maneuvering ever which way to enter and exit. When we entered the ramp and checked in with the ramp controller, we were told that all traffic was being held for us.

"There is a team in place to meet the aircraft", we were told. It looked like it was all coming together, then I realized that once we turned the seat belt sign off, everyone would stand up at once and delay the family from getting off the airplane. As we approached our gate, I asked the co-pilot to tell the ramp controller we were going to stop short of the gate to make an announcement to the passengers. He did that and the ramp controller said, "Take your time."

I stopped the aircraft and set the parking break. I pushed the public address button and said, "Ladies and gentleman, this is your Captain speaking; I have stopped short of our gate to make a special announcement. We have a passenger on board who deserves our honor and respect. His name is Private XXXXX, a soldier who recently lost his life. Private XXXX is under your feet in the cargo hold. Escorting him today is Army Sergeant XXXXX. Also, on board are his father, mother, wife and daughter. Your entire flight crew is asking for all passengers to remain in their seats to allow the family to exit the aircraft first. Thanks you."

We continued the turn to the gate, came to a stop and started our shutdown procedures. A couple of minutes later I opened the cockpit door. I found the two forward flight attendants crying, something you just do not see. I was told that after we came to a stop, every passenger on the aircraft stayed in their seats, waiting for the family to exit the aircraft.

When the family got up and gathered their things, a passenger slowly started to clap his hands. Moments later more passengers joined in and soon the entire aircraft was clapping. Words of "God Bless You,' I'm sorry, thank you, be proud, and other kind words were uttered to the family as they made their way down the aisle and out of the airplane.

They were escorted down to the ramp to finally be with their loved one.

Many of the passengers disembarking thanked me for the announcement I had made. They were just words, I told them, I could say them over and over again, but nothing I say will bring back that brave soldier.

I respectfully ask that all of you reflect on this event and the sacrifices that millions of our men and women have made to ensure our freedom and safety in these UNITED STATES OF AMERICA.

Foot Note:

I know everyone who has served their country who reads this will have tears in their eves, including me. These people die for me and mine, and you and yours, and deserve our honor and respect.

HAIR DRYER

A distinguished young woman on a flight from Ireland asked the Priest beside her, "Father, may I ask a favor?" "Of course my child. What may I do for you?"

"Well, I brought an expensive woman's electronic hair dryer for my mother's birthday that is unopened and well over the Customs limits, and I'm afraid they will confiscate it."

The priest answered, "I would love to help you, dear, but I must warn you; I will not lie."

She said, "With your honest face, Father, no one will question you."

When they got to Customs, she let the priest go ahead of her. The officer asked, "Father, do you have anything to declare?" Father replied, "From the top of my head down to my waist, I have nothing to declare."

The official thought this answer strange, so he asked, "And what do you have to declare from your waist to the floor?" He said, "I have a marvelous instrument designed to be used on a woman, but which is, to date, unused."

Roaring with laughter, the officer said, "Go ahead, Father. Next!!"

GREAT COMEBACKS

Man:	Haven't we met before?
Woman:	Perhaps. I'm the receptionist at the VD Clinic.
Man:	Haven't I seen you someplace before?
Woman:	Yeah, that's why I don't go there anymore.
Man:	Is this seat empty?
Woman:	Yes and this one will be too if you sit down.
Man:	So, wanna go back to my place?
Woman:	Well, I don't know. Will two people fit under the rock?
Man:	Your place or mine?
Woman:	Both. You go to yours and I'll go home to mine.
Man:	I'd like to call you. What's your number?
Woman:	It's in the phone book.
Man:	But I don't know your name.
Woman:	That's in the phone book too.
Man:	So what do you do for a living?
Woman:	I'm a female impersonator.
Man:	Hey, baby, what's your sign?
Woman:	Do Not Enter.
Man:	How do you like your eggs in the morning?
Woman:	Unfertilized.

Man: Hey, come on, we're both here at this bar for the same reason.

Woman: Yeah. Let's pick up some chicks.

Man: I know how to please a woman.

Woman: Then please leave me along.

Man: I want to give myself to you.

Woman: Sorry, I don't accept cheap gifts.

Man: I'd go through anything for you.

Woman: Good. Let's start with your bank account.

Man: I would go to the end of the world for you.

Woman: Yes, but would you stay there?

COURT REPORTER

It can be hard keeping a straight face as a court reporter.

These are from a book called Disorder in the American Courts, and are things people actually said in court, word for word, taken down and now published by court reporters that had the torment of staying calm while these exchanges were actually taking place.

Attorney: What was the first thing your husband said to you that morning?
Witness: He said, "Where am I, Cathy?"
Attorney: And why did that upset you?
Witness: My name is Susan!

Attorney: Are you sexually active?
Witness: No, I just lie there.

Attorney: What gear were you in at the moment of the impact?
Witness: Gucci sweats and Reeboks.

Attorney: This myasthenia gravis, does it affect your memory at all?
Witness: Yes
Attorney: And in what way does it affect your memory?
Witness: I forget.
Attorney: You forget? Can you give us an example of something you forgot?

Attorney: Do you know if your daughter has ever been involved in voodoo?
Witness: We do both.

Attorney: Voodoo?
Witness: We do.
Attorney: You do?
Witness;   Yes, voodoo.

Attorney: Now doctor, isn't it true that when a person dies in his sleep, he doesn't know about it until the next morning?
Witness: Did you actually pas the bar exam?

Attorney: The youngest son, the 20-year old, how old is he?
Witness: He's 20, much like your IQ.

Attorney: Were you present when your picture was taken?
Witness: Are you shitting me?

Attorney: So the date of conception (of the baby) was August 8th?
Witness: Yes.
Attorney: And what were you doing at that time?
Witness: Getting laid.

Attorney: She had three children, right?
Witness: Yes.
Attorney: How many were boys?
Witness: None.
Attorney: Were there any girls?
Witness: Your Honor, I think I need a different attorney. Can I get a new attorney?

Attorney: How was your first marriage terminated?
Witness: By death.
Attorney: And by whose death was it terminated?
Witness: Take a guess.

Attorney: Can you describe the individual?
Witness: He was about medium height and had a beard.

Attorney: Was this a male or female?
Witness: Unless the Circus was in town I'm going with male.

Attorney: Is your appearance here this morning pursuant to a deposition notice which I sent to your attorney?
Witness: No, this is how I dress when I go to work.

Attorney: Doctor, how many of your autopsies have you performed on dead people?
Witness: All of them. The live ones put up too much of a fight.

Attorney: ALL your responses MUST be oral, OK? What school did you go to?
Witness: Oral....

Attorney: Do you recall the time that you examined the body?
Witness: The autopsy started around 8:30 PM.
Attorney: And Mr. Denton was dead at the time?
Witness: If not, he was by the time I finished.

Attorney: Are you qualified to give a urine sample?
Witness: Are you qualified to ask that question?

Attorney: Doctor, before you performed the autopsy, did you check for a pulse?
Witness: No.
Attorney: Did you check for blood pressure.
Witness: No.
Attorney: Did you check for breathing?
Witness: No.
Attorney: So, then it is possible that the patient was alive when you began the autopsy?
Witness: No.
Attorney: How can you be so sure, Doctor?
Witness: Because his brain was sitting on my desk in a jar.

Attorney: I see, but could the patient have still been alive, nevertheless?

Witness: Yes, it is possible that he could have been alive and practicing law.

I FISH

After 35 years of marriage, a husband and wife came for counseling. When asked what the problem was, the wife went into a tirade listing every problem they had ever had in the years they had been married. On and on and on: neglect, lack of intimacy, emptiness, loneliness, feeling unloved, and unlovable, an entire laundry list of unmet needs she had endured.

Finally, after allowing this for a sufficient length of time, the therapist got up, walked around the desk and after asking the wife to stand, he embraced and kissed her long and passionately as her husband watched – with a raised eyebrow. The therapist turned to the husband and said, "This is what your wife needs at least 3 times a week. Can you do this?"

"Well, I can drop her off here on Mondays, Wednesdays, but on Friday's, I fish."

BOB HOPE IN HEAVEN

For those of you too young to remember Bob Hope, ask your Grandparents.

On Turing 70. I still chase women, but only downhill.

On Turning 80. That's the time of your life when even your birthday suit needs pressing.

On Turning 90. You know you're getting old when the candles cost more than the cake.

On Turning 100. I don't feel old, In fact, I don't feel anything until noon. Then it's time for my nap.

On giving up his early Career - Boxing. I ruined my hands in the ring. The referee kept stepping on them.

On Never Winning as Oscar. Welcome to the Academy Awards, or as it called at home, Passover.

On Golf. Golf is my profession. Show business is just to pay the green fees.

On Presidents. I have performed for 12 Presidents and entertained only six.

On Why he Chose Showbiz for his Career. When I was born, the doctor said to my mother, Congratulations, you have an eight pound ham.

On Receiving the Congressional Gold Medal. I feel very humble, but I have the strength of character to fight it.

On His Family's Early Poverty. Four of us slept in the one bed. When it got cold, mother threw on another brother.

On His Six Brothers. That's how I learned to dance. Waiting for the bathroom.

On His Early Failures. I would not have had anything to eat if it wasn't for the stuff audiences threw at me.

On Going to Heaven. I've done benefits for ALL religions. I'd hate to blow the hereafter on a technicality.

AND THANKS FOR THE MEMORIES. A tribute to a man who did make a difference.

HOW TO HAVE THE LAST LAUGH. LOVE THIS COP

A police motorcycle officer stops a driver for shooting through a red light.

The driver if the car is a real bar steward, steps out of the car and comes striding toward the officer, demanding to know why he is being harassed by the Gestapo!

So the officer calmly tells him of the red light violation. The motorist instantly goes on a tirade, questioning the officer's ancestry, sexual orientation, etc., in rather explicit offensive terms.

The tirade goes on without the officer saying a word.

When the officer finishes writing the ticket he puts an "AH" in the lower right corner of the narrative portion of the ticket. He then hands it to the violator for his signature.

The man block signs the ticket angrily, and when presented with his copy points to the "AH" and demands to know what it stands for.

The officer says, "That's so when we go to court, I'll remember that you're an asshole."

Two months later they're in court. The violator has a bad driving record and he has a heap of points and is in danger of losing his license, so he hired an attorney to represent him.

On the stand the officer testifies to seeing the man run through the red light.

Under cross examination the attorney for the defense asks, "Officer is this a reasonable facsimile of the ticket that you issued to my client?

The police officer replies, "Yes, sir, that is the defendant's copy, his signature and mine, same number at the top."

Attorney: "Officer, is there any particular marking or notation on this ticket you don't normally make?"

"Yes, sir, in the lower right corner of the narrative here is an 'AH', underlined."

"What does the 'AH' stand for, officer?"

"Aggressive and hostile, Sir."

"Aggressive and hostile?"

"Yes, sir."

"Officer, are you sure it doesn't stand for asshole?"

"Well, sir, you know your client better than I do."

YOU ARE MEAN!

I am not mean, I am blunt. Which means I will tell you the clear difference between BEING a bit naïve and INCREDIBLY FUCKING STUPID!

FOX NEWS BOWS TO THE PRESSURE!

FOX is already cowering down to the President. In response to President Obama's complaint that FOX News doesn't show enough Bland and Hispanic people on their network.

FOX has announced that they will now air "America's Most Wanted" twice a week.

DARWIN AWARDS

Yes, it's that magical time of the year again when the Darwin Awards are bestowed, honoring the least evolved among us.

Here is this year's winner:

When his.38 caliber revolver failed to fire at his intended victim during a hold-up in Long Beach, California, would-be robber James Elliot did something that can only inspire wonder. He peered down the barrel and tried the trigger again. This time it worked.

And not the honorable mentions:

1. The chef at a hotel in Switzerland lost a finger in a meat cutting machine, and after a little shopping around, submitted a claim to his insurance company. The company expecting negligence sent out one of its men to have a look for himself. He tried the machine and he also lost a finger. The insurance company approved the chef's claim.

2. A man, who shoveled snow for an hour to clear a space for his car during a blizzard in Chicago, returned with his vehicle to find a woman had taken the space. Understandably, he shot her.

3. An American teenager was in the hospital recovering from serious head wounds received from an oncoming train. When asked how he received the injuries, the lad told police that he was simply trying to see how close he could get his head to a moving train before he was hit.

4. A man walked into a Louisiana Circle-K, put a $20 bill on the counter and asked for change. When the clerk opened the

cash drawer, the man pulled a gun and asked for all the cash in the register, which the clerk promptly provided. The man took the cash from the clerk and fled, leaving the $20 bill on the counter. The total amount of cash he got from the drawer … $15.

5. (Question: If someone points a gun at you and gives you money, is a crime committed.)

6. Seems an Arkansas guy wanted some beer pretty badly. He decided that he'd just throw a cinder block through a liquor store window, grab some booze and run. So he lifted the cinder block and heaved it over his head at the window. The cinder block bounced back and hit the would-be thief on the head, knocking him unconscious. The liquor store window was made of Plexiglas. The whole event was caught on videotape.

7. As a female shopper exited a New York convenience store, a man grabbed her purse and ran. The clerk called 911 immediately, and the woman was able to give them a detailed description of the snatcher. Within minutes, the police apprehended the snatcher. They put him in the car and drove back to the store. The thief was taken out of the car and told to stand there for a positive ID. To which he replied, "Yes, officer, that's her. That's the lady I stole the purse from."

8. The Ann Arbor News crime column reported that a man walked into a Burger King in Ypsilanti, Michigan at 5 A.M., flashed a gun, and demanded cash. The clerk turned him down because he said he couldn't open the cash register without a food order. When the man ordered onion rings, the clerk said they weren't available for breakfast… The frustrated gunman walked away.

9. When a man attempted to siphon gasoline from a motor home parked on a Seattle street by sucking on a hose, he got much more than he bargained for. Police arrived at the scene to find a very sick man curled up next to a motor home near spilled sewage. A police spokesman said that the man admitted to trying to steal gasoline, but he plugged his siphon hose into the motor home's sewage take by mistake. The owner of the vehicle declined to press charges saying that it was the best laugh he'd ever had and the perp had been punished enough!

Remember…they walk among us and they can reproduce!

OLDER MEN SCAM

Women often receive warnings about protecting themselves at the mall and in dark parking lots, etc. This is the first warning I have seen for men.

A "heads up" for those men who may be regular customers at Lowe's, home depot, Costco, or even Wal-Mart. This one caught me totally by surprise. Over the last month I became a victim f a clever scam while out shopping. Simply going out to get supplies has turned out to be quite traumatic. Don't be naïve enough to think it couldn't happen to you or your friends.

Here's how the scam works:

Two nice-looking, college-aged girls will come over to your car or truck as you are packing your purchases into your vehicle. They both start wiping your windshield with a rag and Windex, with their breasts almost falling out of their skimpy t-shirts. (It's impossible not to look). When you thank them and offer them a tip, they say 'No' but instead ask for a ride to McDonald's.

You agree and they climb into the vehicle. On the way, they start undressing. Then one of them starts crawling all over you, while the other one steals your wallet.

I had my wallet stolen Feb. 4th, 9th, 10th, twice on the 15th, 17th, 20th, 24th and 29th. Also March 1st and 4th, twice the 8th, 16th, 23rd, 26th and 27th, and very likely again this coming weekend.

So tell your friends to be careful. What a horrible way to take advantage of us older men. Warn your friends to be vigilant.

Wal-Mart has wallets on sale for $2.99 each. I found even cheaper ones for $.99 at the Dollar Store and bought them out in three of their stores.

Although you never get to eat at McDonald's, I've already lost 11 pounds just running back and forth from Lowe's, to Home Depot, to Costco, etc.

So please, send this on to all the older men that you know and warn them to be on the lookout for this scam. (The best times are just before lunch, and around 4:30 in the afternoon.)

HI MY FRIEND

One day I had lunch with some friends. Jim, a short, balding golfer type about 80 years old came along with them all in all, a pleasant bunch. When the menus were presented, we ordered salads, sandwiches, and soups, except for Jim who said, "Ice Cream, please. Two scoops, chocolate.

I wasn't sure my ears heard right, and the others were aghast. "Along with heated apple pie" Jim added, completely unabashed.

We tried to act quite nonchalant, as if people did this all the time. But when our orders were brought out, I didn't enjoy mine. I couldn't take my eyes off Jim as his pie a-la-mode went down. The other guys couldn't believe it either. They ate their lunches silently and grinned.

The next time I went out to eat, I called and invited Jim. I lunched on white meat tuna. He ordered a parfait. I smiled. He asked if he amused me and I answered, "Yes. You do, but also you confuse me. How come you order rich desserts, while I feel I must be sensible?" He laughed and said, "I taste all that is possible.

"I try to eat the food I need, and do the things I should. But life's so short, my friend, I hate missing out on something good."

"This year I realized how old I was. (He grinned). I haven't been this old before. So before I die, I've got to try those things that for years I had ignored. I haven't smelled all the flowers yet. There are too many trout streams I haven't fished. There's more fudge sundaes to wolf down and kites to be flown overhead. There are too many golf courses I haven't played. I've not laughed at all the jokes. I've missed a lot of sporting events and potato chips and cokes."

"I want to wade again in water to feel ocean spray on my face. I want to sit in a country church once more and thank God for His grace. I want peanut butter every day spread on my morning toast. I want un-timed long distance call to folks I love the most."

"I haven't cried at all the movies yet, or walked in the morning rain. I need to feel wind on my face. I want to be in love again."

So if I choose to have dessert, instead of having dinner, then should I die before night fall, I'd say I died a winner, because I missed out on nothing. I filled my heart's desire. I had that final chocolate mousse before my life expired."

With that, I called the waitress over. "I've changed my mind," I said. "I want what he is having; only add some more whipped cream!"

HYMN #365

A minister was completing a temperance sermon. With great emphasis he said. "If I had all the beer in the world, I'd take it and pour it into the river."

With even greater emphasis he said, "And if I had all the wine in the world, I'd take it and pour it into the river."

And then finally, shaking his fist in the air, he said, "And if I had all the whiskey in the world, I'd take it and pour it into the river."

Sermon completed, he sat down. The choir leader stood very cautiously and announced with a smile, nearly laughing, "For our closing song, let us sing hymn #365, "Shall We Gather at the River."

See you at the river!

WHAT IS THE SMALLEST CALIBER YOU TRUST TO PROTECT YOURSELF?

The Beretta Jetfire:

I remember one time while hiking with my girlfriend in northern Alberta and out of nowhere came this huge brown bear charging us and was she ever mad. We must have been near one of her cubs. Anyway, if I had not had my little Jetfire, I would not be here today.

Just one shot to my girlfriend's knee cap was all it took…the bear got her and I was able to escape by just walking at a brisk pace.

It's one of the best pistols in my collection…

31 THINGS YOU'LL NEVER HEAR SOUTHERN BOYS SAY

1. When I retire, I'm moving North.
2. Oh, I just couldn't, she's only sixteen.
3. I'll take Shakespeare for 1000 Alex.
4. Duct tape won't fix that.
5. Come to think of it, I'll have a Heineken.
6. We don't keep firearms in this house.
7. You can't feed that to the dog.
8. No kids in the back of the pickup, it's just not safe.
9. Wrestling is fake.
10. We're vegetarians.
11. Do you think my gut is too big?
12. I'll have grapefruit and grapes instead of biscuits and gravy…
13. Honey, we don't need another dog.
14. Who gives a damn who won the Civil War?
15. Give me the small bag of pork rinds.
16. Too many deer heads detract from the décor.
17. I just couldn't find a thing at Wal-Mart today.
18. Trim the fat off that steak.
19. Cappuccino tastes better than espresso.
20. The tires on that truck are too big.
21. I've got it all on the C: Drive.

22. Unsweetened tea tastes better.

23. My fiancé, Bobby Jo, is registered at Tiffany's.

24. I've got two cases of Zima for the Super Bowl.

25. Checkmate.

26. She's too young to be wearing a bikini.

27. Hey, here's an episode of "Hee Haw" that we haven't seen.

28. I don't have a favorite college team.

29. "You Guys".

30. Those shorts ought to be a little longer, Betty Mae.

31. Nope, no more beer for me. I'm driving a whole busload of us down to the festival.

BLACK AND WHITE TV

This is for my ancient friends who will all appreciate it and to some of my younger friends so they will know what they missed out on.

- Black and White (under age 40 you won't understand)
- You could hardly see for all the snow.
- Spread the rabbit ears as far as they go.
- Pull a chair up to the TV set.
- 'Good Night David. Good Night Chet'.
- My Mom used to cut chicken, chop eggs and spread mayo on the same cutting board with the same knife, and no bleach, but we didn't seem to get food poisoning.
- My mom used to defrost hamburger on the counter and I used to eat it raw sometimes, too.
- Our school sandwiches were wrapped in wax pager in a brown pager bay, not in ice pack coolers, but I can't remember getting E. coli.
- Almost all of us would have rather gone swimming in the lake instead of a pristine pool (talk about boring), no beach closures then.
- We all took gym, not PE…and risked permanent injury with a pair of high top Keds (only worn in gym) instead of having cross-training athletic shoes with air cushion soles and built in light reflectors. I can't recall any injuries but they must have happened because they tell us how much safer we are now.

- Flunking gym was not an option...Even for stupid kids! I guess PE must be much harder than gym.

- We must have had horribly damaged psyches. What an archaic health system we had then. Remember school nurses? Ours wore a hat and everything.

- I thought that I was supposed to accomplish something before I was allowed to be proud of myself.

- I just can't recall how bored we were without computers, Play Stations, Nintendo, X-Box or 270 digital TV cable stations.

- Oh yeah...And where was the Benadryl and sterilization kit when I got that bee sting? I could have been killed!

- We played king on the mountain, on piles of gravel left on vacant construction sites, and when we got hurt, Mom pulled out the $.48 bottle of mercurochrome (kids liked it because it didn't sting like iodine did) and then we got our butt spanked. Now it's a trip to the emergency room, followed by a 10-day dose of a $49 bottle of antibiotics, and then Mom calls the attorney to sue the contractor for leaving a horribly vicious pile of gravel where it was such a threat.

- We didn't act up at the neighbor's house either; because if we did we got our butt spanked there and then when we got home our butt spanked again.

- I recall Donny Reynolds from next door coming over and doing his tricks on the front stoop, just before he fell off. Little did his Mom know that she could have owned our house. Instead, she picked him up and swatted him for being such a goof. It was a neighborhood run amuck.

- To top it off, not a single person I knew had ever been told that they were from a dysfunctional family. How could we possibly have known that? Now we need group therapy and anger management classes. We were obviously so duped by so many societal ills, that we didn't even notice that the entire country wasn't taking Prozac!

How did we ever survive?

Love to all of us who shared this era; and to all who didn't, sorry for what you missed.

FOUR RULES TO REMEMBER IN LIFE

1. Money cannot buy happiness, but it's more comfortable to cry in a Mercedes than on a bicycle.

2. Forgive your enemy, but remember the bastard's name.

3. Help someone when they are in trouble and they will remember you when they're in trouble again.

4. Many people are alive only because it's illegal to shoot them.

BEST DIVORCE LETTER EVER!

Dear Wife:

I'm writing you this letter to tell you that I'm leaving you forever. I've been a good man to you for 27 years and I have nothing to show for it.

These last two weeks have been hell. Your boss called to tell me that you quit your job today and that was the last straw. Last week, you came home and didn't even notice I had a new haircut, had cooked your favorite meal and even wore a brand new pair of silk boxers. You ate in 2 minutes and went straight to sleep after watching all of your soaps. You don't want sex or anything that connects us as husband and wife. Either you're cheating on me or you don't love me anymore; whatever the case, I'm gone.

Your
Ex-Husband

Dear Ex-Husband:

Nothing has made my day more than receiving your letter. It's true you and I have been married for 27 years, although a good man is a far cry from what you've been. I watch my soaps so much to try to drown out your constant whining and griping. Too bad that doesn't work.
I DID notice when you got a hair cut last week, but the first thing that came to mind was 'You look just like a girl!' Since my mother raised me not to say anything if you can say something nice, I didn't comment. And when you cooked my favorite meal, you must have

gotten me confused with MY SISTER, because I stopped eating pork 7 years ago.

About those new silk boxers: I turned away from you because the $49.99 price tag was still on them and I prayed it was a coincidence that my sister had just borrowed $50 from me that morning. After all of this, I still love you and felt we could work it out. So when I hit the lotto for $10 million, I quit my job and bought us 2 tickets to Jamaica, but when I got home you were gone.

Everything happens for a reason, I guess. I hope you have the fulfilling life you always wanted. My lawyer said that the letter you wrote ensures you won't get a dime from me.

So take care.

Signed,
Your Ex-Wife, Rich as Hell and Free!

P.S. I don't know if I ever told you this, but my sister Carla was born Carl. I hope that's not a problem.

OUR NATIONAL PASTIME
BY DAVE BARRY

This Dave Barry column was originally published March 31, 1996.
As I ponder the start of yet another baseball season, what is left of
my mind drifts back to the fall of 1960, when I was as student at
Harold C. Crittenden Junior High ("Where the Leaders of tomorrow
Are Developing the Acne of Today"). The big baseball story that
year was the World Series between the New York Yankees and the
Pittsburg Pirates. Today, for sound TV viewership reasons, all World
Series games are played after most people, including many of the
players, have gone to bed. But in 1960 the games had to be played in
the daytime, because the electric light had not been invented yet.
Also, back then the players and owners had not yet discovered the
marketing benefits of sporadically canceling entire seasons.

The result was that in those days young people were actually
interested in baseball, unlike today's young people, who are much
more interested in basketball, football, soccer and downloading dirty
pictures from the Internet. But in my youth, baseball ruled. Almost
all of us boys played in Little League, a character-building
experience that helped me develop a personal relationship with God.
"God," I would say, when I was standing in deep right field- the
coach put me in right field only because it was against the rules to
put me in Sweden, where I would have gone less damage to the
team – 'please please PLEASE don't let the ball come to me."

But of course God enjoys a good prank as much as the next
infallible deity, which is why, when He heard me pleading with Him,
He always took time out from His busy schedule to make sure the
next batter hit a towering blast that would, upon re-entering the
Earth's atmosphere, come down directly where I would have been

standing, if I had stood still, which I never did. I lunged around cluelessly in frantic, random circles, so that the ball always landed a minimum of 40 feet from where I wound up standing, desperately thrusting out my glove, which was a Herb Score model that, on my coach's recommendation, I had treated with neat's-foot oil so it would be supple. Looking back, I feel bad that innocent neats had to sacrifice their feet for the sake of my glove. I would have been just as effective, as a fielder, if I'd been wearing a bowling shoe on my hand, or a small aquarium. But even though I stunk at it, I was into baseball. My friends and I collected baseball cards, the kind that came in a little pack with a dusty, pale-pink rectangle of linoleum-textured World War II surplus bubble gum that was far less edible than the cards themselves. Like every other male my age who collected baseball cards as a boy, I now firmly believe that at one time I had the original rookie cards of Mickey Mantle, Jackie Robinson, Ty Cobb, Babe Ruth, Jim Thorpe, Daniel Boone, Goliath, etc., and that I'd be able to sell my collection for $163 million today except my mom threw them out.

My point is that we cared deeply about baseball back then, which meant that we were passionate about the 1960 Pirates-Yankees World Series matchup. My class was evenly divided between those who were Pirate fans and those who were complete morons. (I never have cared for the Yankees, and for a very sound reason: The Yankees are evil.)

We followed every pitch of every game. It wasn't easy, because the weekday games started when we were still in school, which for some idiot reason was not called off for the World Series. This meant that certain students – I am not naming names, because even now, it could go on our Permanent records – had to carry concealed transistor radios to class. A major reason why the Russians got so far ahead of us, academically, during the Cold War is that while Russian students were listening to their teachers explain the cosine, we were listening, via concealed earphones, to announcers explain how a bad hop nailed Tony Kubek in the throat.

That series went seven games, and I vividly remember how it ended. School was out for the day, and I was heading home, pushing my bike up a steep hill, listening to my cheapo little radio, my eyes staring vacantly ahead, my mind locked on the game. A delivery truck came by, and the driver stopped and asked if he could listen. Actually, he more or less told me he was going to listen; I said OK. The truck driver turned out to be a rabid Yankee fan. The game was very close, and we stood on opposite sides of my bike for the final two innings, rooting for opposite teams, him chain-smoking Lucky Strike cigarettes, both of us hanging on every word coming out of my tinny little speaker.

And of course if you were around back then and did not live in Russia, you know what happened: God, in a sincere effort to make up for all those fly balls he directed toward me in Little League, had Bill Mazeroski - Bill Mazeroski! – hit a home run to win it for the Pirates. I was insane with joy. The truck driver was devastated. But I will never forget what he said to me. He looked me square in the eye, one baseball fan to another, after a tough but fair fight - and he said a seriously bad word. Several, in fact. Then he got in his truck and drove away. That was the best game I ever saw.

ABOUT THE WRITER
Dave Berry is a Pulitzer winning humor columnist for the Miami Herald.

WHY MEN ARE NEVER DEPRESSED

Men are just happier people—what do you expect from such simple creatures?

- Your last name stays put.
- The garage is all yours.
- Wedding plans take care of themselves.
- Chocolate is just another snack…
- You can be President.
- You can never be pregnant.
- You can wear a white T-shirt to a water park.
- You can wear NO shirt to a water park.
- Car mechanics tell you the truth.
- The world is your urinal.
- You never have to drive to another gas station restroom because this one is just too icky.
- You don't have to stop and think of which way to turn a nut on a bolt.
- Same work, more pay.
- Wrinkles add character.
- Wedding dress $5,000. Tux rental - $100.
- People never stare at your chest when you're talking to them.
- New shoes don't cut, blister, or mangle you feet.
- One mood all the time.

- Phone conversations are over in 30 seconds flat.

- You know stuff about tanks.

- A five-day vacation requires only one suitcase.

- You can open all your own jars.

- You get extra credit for the slightest act of thoughtfulness.

- If someone forgets to invite you, he or she can still be your friend.

- Your underwear is $8.95 for a three-pack.

- Three pairs of shoes are more than enough.

- Your almost never have strap problems in public.

- You are unable to see wrinkles in your clothes.

- Everything on your face stays its original color.

- The same hairstyle lasts for years, even decades.

- You only have to shave your face and neck.

- You can play with toys all your life.

- One wallet and one pair of shoes - - one color for all seasons.

- You can wear shorts no matter how your legs look.

- You can 'do' your nails with a pocket knife.

- You have freedom of choice concerning growing a mustache.

- You can do Christmas shopping for 25 relatives on December 24 in 25 minutes.

MEN ARE JUST HAPPIER PEOPLE

Nicknames - If Laura, Kate and Sarah go out for lunch, they will call each other Laura, Kate and Sarah. If Mike, Dave and John go out, they will affectionately refer to each other as Fat Boy, Bubba and WWWildman.

Eating Out - When the bill arrives, Mike, Dave and John will each throw in $20, even though it's only for $32.50. None of them will have anything smaller and none will actually admit they want change back. When the girls get their bill, out come the pocket calculators.

Money - A man will pay $2 for a $1 item he needs. A woman will pay $1 for a $2 item that she doesn't need but it's on sale.

Bathrooms - A man has six items in his bathroom" toothbrush and toothpaste, shaving cream, razor, a bar of soap, and a towel. The average number of items in the typical woman's bathroom is 337. A man would not be able to identify more than 20 of these items.

Arguments - A woman has the last word in any argument. Anything a man says after that is the beginning of a new argument.

Future - A woman worries about the future until she gets a husband. A man never worries about the future until he gets a wife.

Marriage - A woman marries a man expecting he will change, but he doesn't. A man marries a woman expecting that she won't change, but she does.

Dressing Up - A woman will dress up to go shopping, water the plants, empty the trash, answer the phone, read a book, and get the mail. A man will dress up for weddings and funerals.

Natural - Men wake up as good-looking as they went to bed. Women somehow deteriorate during the night.

Offspring - Ah children. A woman knows all about her children. She knows about dentist appointments and romances, best friends, favorite foods, secret fears and hopes and dreams. A man is vaguely aware of some short people living in the house.

Thought for the Day - A married man should forget his mistakes. There's no use in two people remembering the same thing.

So, send this to the women who have a sense of humor and who can handle it … and to the men who will enjoy reading it.

DIFFERENCE BETWEEN MAN AND WOMEN
BY GEORGE CARLIN

Here's all you have to know about men and women: women are crazy, men are stupid.

And the main reason women are crazy is that men are stupid.

Bonus: Chapter of Sayings

WE'RE ALL SIGNIFICANT

During my second month of nursing school, our professor game us a pop quiz. I was a conscientious student and had breezed through the questions, until I read the last one: "What is the first name of the woman who cleans the school?" Surely this was some kind of joke. I had seen the cleaning woman several times. She was tall, dark-haired and in her 50's, but how would I know her name? I handed in my paper, leaving the last question blank. Just before class ended, one student asked if the last question would count toward our quiz grade. "Absolutely," said the professor. "In your careers, you will meet many people. All are significant. They deserve your attention and care, even if all you do is smile and say 'hello'." I've never forgotten that lesson. I've also never forgotten her name was Dorothy.

SHAKE IT OFF AND TAKE A STEP UP

One day a farmer's donkey fell down into a well. The animal cried for hours as the farmer tried to figure out what to do. Finally he decided the animal was old and the well needed to be covered up anyway; it just wasn't worth it to retrieve the donkey. He invited all his neighbors to come over and help him.

They all grabbed a shovel and began to shovel dirt into the well. At first, the donkey realized what was happening and cried horribly. Then, to everyone's amazement, he quieted down. A few shovel loads later, the farmer finally looked down the well and was astonished at what he saw. With every shovel of dirt that hit his back, the donkey was going something amazing. He would shake it off and take a step up.

As the farmer's neighbors continued to shovel dirt on top of the animal he would shake it off and take a step up. Pretty soon, everyone was amazed as the donkey stepped up over the edge of the well and trotted off!

Life is going to shovel dirt on you, all kinds of dirt. The trick is getting out of the well is to shake it off and take a step up. Each of our troubles is a stepping-stone. We can get out of the deepest wells just by not stopping, never giving up!

WISDOM OF WILL ROGERS

- Letting the cat out of the bag is a whole lot easier than putting it back in.

- If you're riding ahead of the herd, take a look back every now and then to make sure it's still there.

- If you get to thinking you're a person of some influence, try ordering somebody else's dog around.

- After eating an entire bull, a mountain lion felt so good he started roaring. He kept it up until a hunter came along and shot him. The moral: When you're full of bull, keep your mouth shut.

- If you find yourself in a hole, the first thing to do is stop digging.

- It doesn't take a genius to spot a goat in a flock of sheep.

- The quickest way to double your money is to fold it over and put it back in your pocket.

- Don't squat with your spurs on.

- Good judgment comes from experience, and a lot of that comes form bad judgment.

- Never miss a good chance to shut up.

DON'T WORRY, BE HAPPY

- Live below your means.
- Say "hello" to strangers.
- Remember names.
- Compliment at least three people a day.
- Be cheerful even when you don't feel like it.
- When you enter a room, let your first words be positive.
- Keep your promise.
- Be tough in spirit but tender in heart.
- Search for wisdom rather than striving for things.
- Be kinder than necessary.
- Remember that the greatest gift you can give is appreciation.
- Remember to leave thing better than you found them.
- Remember that winners do what losers won't.
- Remember not to give up. Miracles happen.
- Don't rain on anyone's parade.
- Never pass up an opportunity to say "I love you." It may be your last.

21 SUGGESTIONS FOR SUCCESS

1. Marry the right person. This one decision will determine 90% of your happiness or misery.

2. Work at something you enjoy and that's worthy of your time and talent.

3. Give people more than they expect and do it cheerfully.

4. Become the most positive and enthusiastic person you know.

5. Be forgiving of yourself and others.

6. Be generous.

7. Have a grateful heart.

8. Persistence, persistence, persistence.

9. Discipline yourself to save money on even the most modest salary.

10. Treat everyone you meet like you want to be treated.

11. Commit yourself to constant improvement.

12. Commit yourself to quality.

13. Understand that happiness is not based on possessions, power or prestige, but on relationships with people you love and respect.

14. Be loyal.

15. Be honest.

16. Be a self-starter.

17. Be decisive even if it means you'll sometimes be wrong.

18. Stop blaming others. Take responsibility for every area of your life.

19. Be bold and courageous. When you look back on your life, you'll regret the things you didn't do more than the ones you did.

20. Take good care of those you love.

21. Don't do anything that wouldn't make your Mom proud.

WORDS OF WISDOM

- Make friends before you need them.
- The road to success is always under construction.
- If you must cry over spilled milk, please try to condense it.
- Skate to where the puck is going to be, not where is has been.
- Live so that when your children think of fairness, caring, and integrity, they think of you.
- Listening is not waiting to talk.
- All of the slow rabbits done been shot.
- Be sure you know your customer's "true" personality.
- Trust your hopes, not your fears.

THINGS WE LEARN FROM OUR DOGS

- Avoid biting when a simple growl will do.
- Take naps and stretch before rising.

VERBS TO REMEMBER

- Trust
- Learn
- Communicate
- Enable
- Build

THOUGHTS TO START YOUR DAY

Gardening Rule: When weeding, the best way to make sure you are removing a weed and not a valuable plant is to pull on it. If it comes out of the ground easily, it is a valuable plant.

The easiest way to find something lost around the house is to buy a replacement.

Never take life seriously. Nobody gets out alive anyway.

There are two kinds of pedestrians - - The quick and the dead.

Life is sexually transmitted.

An unbreakable toy is useful for breaking other toys.

If quitters never win, and winners never quit, then who is the fool who said "Quit while you're ahead"?

Health is merely the slowest possible rate at which one can die.

The only difference between a rut and a grave is the depth.

Get the last word in: Apologize.

Give a person a fish and you feed them for a day; teach that person to use the Internet and they won't bother you for four weeks.
Some people are like Slinkies … not really good for anything, but you still can't help but smile when you see one tumble down the stairs.

Health nuts are going to feel stupid someday, lying in hospitals dying of nothing.

Have you noticed since everyone has a camcorder these days no one talks about seeing UFO's like they use to?

Whenever I feel blue, I start breathing again.

All of us could take a lesson from the weather! It pays no attention to criticism.

Why does a slight tax increase cost you two hundred dollars and a substantial tax cut caves you thirty cents.

In the 60's people took acid to make the world weird. Now the world is weird and people take Prozac to make it normal.

Politics is supposed to be the second oldest profession. I have come to realize that it bears a very close resemblance to the first.

How is it one careless match can start a forest fire, but it takes a whole box to start a campfire?

And the No 1 Thought for the Day:
You read about all these terrorists - - most of them came here legally, but they hung around on these expired visas, some for as long as 10 – 15 years. Now, compare that to Blockbuster; you are two days late with a video and those people are all over you. Let's put Blockbuster in charge of immigration.

Never sweat the idiot who has left the room.
Instead, worry about the ones who remain.
—Rush Limbaugh

OLDIES BUT GOODIES - WORDS OF WISDOM

- Tact is the ability to see others as they wish to be seen.
- Live as you wish your kids would.
- Too often people mistake being busy for achieving goals.
- If you don't have time to do something right, when will you have time to do it over?
- Listening is not waiting to talk.
- We are what we repeatedly do. Excellence then is not an act, but a habit.
- Diplomacy is the art of letting someone else get your way.
- A smile is an inexpensive way to improve your looks.
- Remember that overnight success usually takes about fifteen years.

WORDS OF WISDOM

1. Learn to disagree without being disagreeable. It's all right to be assertive, but not aggressive, abusive, or abrasive.

2. When someone says something with which you disagree, try not to be judgmental.

3. Maintain eye contact when greeting people, and shake their hand. (Touching is important.)

4. Be kind and generous to everyone.

5. Remember that civility is a sign of strength, not weakness.

6. Speak softly. (People tune out loud, angry voices.)

7. Saving face is important. Give your opponent the opportunity to withdraw.

8. Your attitude is more important than your aptitude.

9. Mutual respect is the key to avoiding conflicts.

10. Give the other person a chance to be heard without interrupting.

11. The shortest distance between two people is a smile.

12. The joy of soaring almost always begins with the fear of falling.

KIMO'S MAUI RULES

- Never judge a day by the weather.
- The best things in life aren't things.
- Tell the truth – there's less to remember.
- Speak softly and wear a loud shirt.
- Goals are deceptive – the un-aimed arrow never misses.
- He who dies with the most toys – still dies.
- Age is relative – when you're over the hill, you pick up speed.
- There are 2 ways to be rich – make more and desire less
- Beauty is internal – looks mean nothing.
- No rain – No Rainbow.

THE MAYONNAISE JAR AND COFFEE

When things in your life seem almost too much to handle, when 24 hours in a day are not enough, remember the mayonnaise jar … and the coffee …

A professor stood before his philosophy class and had some items in front of him. When the class began, wordlessly, he picked up a very large and empty mayonnaise jar and proceeded to fill it with golf balls. He then asked the students if the jar was full. They agreed that it was.

The professor then picked u a box of pebbles and poured them into the far. He shook the jar lightly. The pebbles rolled into the open areas between the golf balls. He then asked the students again if the jar was full. They agreed it was.

The professor next picked up a box of sand and poured it into the jar. Of course, the sand filled up everything else. He asked once more if the far was full. The students responded with a unanimous "yes."

The professor then produced two cups of coffee from under the table and poured the entire contents into the jar, effectively filling the empty space between the sand. The students laughed.

"Now," said the professor, as the laughter subsided, "I want you to recognize that this jar represents your life. The golf balls are the important things – your God, family, your children, your health, your friends and you favorite passions. Things that if everything else was lost and only they remained, you life would still be full.

The pebbles are the other things that matter like your job, your house, and your car. The sand is everything else-the small stuff. If you put the sand into the far first," he continued, "there is no room for the pebbles or the golf balls. The same goes for life. If you spend all your time and energy on the small stuff, you will never have room for the tings that are important to you."

"Pay attention to the things that are critical to your happiness. Play with your children. Take time to get medical checkups. Take your partner out to dinner. Play. Take care of your friends. There will always be time to clean the house and fix the disposal. Take care of the golf balls first, the things that really matter. Set your priorities. The rest is just sand."

One of the students raised her hand and inquired what the coffee represented. The professor smiled. "I'm glad you asked. It just to show you that no matter how full your life may seem, there's always room for a couple of cups of coffee with a friend." With that he dismissed the class.

WORDS WITH MEANING

- Give people more than they expect and do it cheerfully.

- Marry a man/woman you love to talk to. As you get older, their conversational skills will be as important as any other.

- Don't believe all you hear, spend all you have or sleep all you want.

- When you say, "I love you," mean it.

- When you say, "I'm sorry," look the person in the eye.

- Be engaged at least six months before you get married.

- Believe in love at first sight.

- Never laugh at anyone's dreams. People who don't have dreams don't have much.

- Love deeply and passionately. You might get hurt but it's the only way to live life completely.

- In disagreements, fight fairly. No name-calling.

- Don't judge people by their relatives.

- Talk slowly but think quickly.

- When someone asks you a question you don't want to answer, smile and ask, "Why do you want to know?"

- Remember that great love and great achievements involve great risk.

- Say 'bless you" when you hear someone sneeze.

- When you lose, don't lose the lesson.

- Remember the three R's: Respect for self; Respect for others; and responsibility for all your actions.

- Don't let a little dispute injure a great friendship.

- When you realize you've made a mistake, take immediate steps to correct it.

- Smile when picking up the phone. The caller will hear it in your voice.

- Spend one time alone.

THE GREATEST AND MOST....

- The most destructive habit: Worry
- The greatest joy: Giving
- The greatest loss: Loss of self-respect
- The most satisfying work: Helping others
- The ugliest personality trait: Selfishness
- The most endangered species: Dedicated leaders
- Our greatest natural resource: Our youth
- The greatest "shot in the arm": Encouragement
- The greatest problem to overcome: Fear
- The most effective sleeping pill: Peace of mind
- The most crippling failure disease: Excuses
- The most powerful force in life: Love
- The most dangerous pariah: A gossiper
- The world's most incredible computer: The brain
- The worst thing to be without : Hope
- The deadliest weapon: The tongue
- The two most power-filled words: "I Can"
- The greatest asset: Faith
- The most worthless emotion: Self-pity
- The most beautiful attire: SMILE !
- The most prized possession: Integrity
- The most powerful channel of communication: Prayer
- The most contagious spirit: Enthusiasm

GOD SAYS

I asked God to take away my habit. God said, no. It is not for me to take away, but for you to give it up.

I asked God to make my handicapped child whole. God said, no. His spirit is whole, his body is only temporary.

I asked God to grant me patience. God said, no. Patience is a byproduct of tribulations; it isn't granted, it is learned.

I asked God to give me happiness. God said, no. I give you blessings; happiness is up to you.

I asked God to spare me pain. God said, no. Suffering draws you apart from worldly cares and beings you closer to me.

I asked Got to make my spirit grow. God said, no. You must grow on your own, but I will prune you to make you fruitful.

I asked God for all things that I might enjoy life. God said, no. I will give you life, so that you may enjoy all things.

I asked God to help me love others, as much as He loves me. God said, .. Ahhhh, finally you have an idea.

This day is yours, don't throw it away

To the world you might be one person, but to one person you just might be the world.

LESSONS OF LIFE

This was written by Regina Brett of The Plain Dealer Newspaper in Cleveland, Ohio.

To celebrate growing older, I once wrote the 45 lessons life taught me. It is the most-requested column I've ever written. My odometer rolls over to 70 in August, so here goes:

1. Life isn't fair, but it's still good.
2. When in doubt, just take the next small step.
3. Life is too short to waste time hating anyone.
4. Don't take yourself so seriously. No one else does.
5. Pay off your credit cards every month.
6. You don't have to win every argument. Agree to disagree.
7. Cry with someone, It's more healing than crying alone.
8. It's OK to get angry with God. He can take it.
9. Save for retirement starting with your first paycheck.
10. When it comes to chocolate, resistance is futile.
11. Make peace with your past so it won't screw up the present.
12. It's OK to let your children see you cry.
13. Don't compare your life to others'. You have no idea what their journey is all about.
14. If a relationship has to be a secret, you shouldn't be in it.
15. Everything can change in the blink of an eye. But don't worry; God never blinks.
16. Take a deep breath. It calms the mind.

17. Get rid of anything that isn't useful, beautiful or joyful.

18. Whatever doesn't kill you really does make you stronger.

19. It's never too late to have a happy childhood. But the second one is up to you and no one else.

20. When it comes to going after what you love in life, don't take no for an answer.

21. Burn the candles, use the nice sheets, and wear the fancy lingerie. Don't save it for a special occasion. Today is special.

22. Over prepare, then go with the flow.

23. Be eccentric now. Don't wait for old age to wear purple.

24. The most important sex organ is the brain.

25. No one is in charge of your happiness, except you.

26. Frame every so-called disaster with these words: "In five years, will this matter?"

27. Always choose life.

28. Forgive everyone everything.

29. What other people think of you is none of your business.

30. Time heals almost everything. Give time.

31. However good or bad a situation is, it will change.

32. Your job won't take care of you when you are sick. Your friends will. Stay in touch.

33. Believe in miracles.

34. God loves you because of whom God is, not because of anything you did or didn't do.

35. Don't audit life. Show up and make the most of it now.

36. Growing old beats the alternative --- dying young.

37. Your children get only one childhood. Make it memorable.

38. All that truly matters in the end is that you loved.

39. Get outside every day. Miracles are waiting everywhere.

40. If we all threw our problems in a pile and was everyone else's, we'd grab ours back.

41. Envy is a waste of time. You already have all you need.

42. The best is yet to come.

43. No matter how you feel, get up, dress up and show up.

44. Yield.

45. Life isn't tied with a bow, but it's still a gift.

FROM ABRAHAM LINCOLN

You cannot bring about prosperity by discouraging thrift. You cannot strengthen the weak by weakening the strong. You cannot help the wage earner by pulling down the wage payer. You cannot further the brotherhood of man by encouraging class hated. You cannot help the poor by destroying the rich. You cannot keep out of trouble by spending more than you earn. You cannot build character and courage by taking away man's initiative and independence. You cannot help men permanently by doing for them what they could and should do for themselves.

—Abraham Lincoln.

PARADOX OF OUR TIME IN HISTORY

What a difference a sad event in someone's life makes. George Carlin's wife recently died. Isn't it amazing that George Carlin – comedian of the 70's and 80's – could write something so very eloquent… and so very appropriate.

The paradox of our time in history is that we have taller buildings, but shorter tempers, wider Freeways, but narrower viewpoints. We spend more, but have less, we buy more, but enjoy less. We have bigger houses and smaller families, more conveniences, but less time. We have more degrees, but less sense, more knowledge, but less judgment, more experts, yet more problems, more medicine, but less wellness.

We drink too much, smoke too much, spend too recklessly, laugh too little, drive too fast, get too angry, stay up too late, get up too tired, read too little, watch TV too much, and pray too seldom.

We have multiplied our possessions, but reduced our values. We talk to much, love too seldom, and hate too often.

We've learned how to make a living, but not a life. We've added years to life not life to years. We've been all the way to the moon and back, but have trouble crossing the street to meet a new neighbor. We conquered outer space, but not inner space. We've done larger things, but not better things.

We've cleaned up the air, but polluted the soul. We've conquered the atom, but not our prejudice. We write more, but learn less. We plan more, but accomplish less. We've learned to rush, but not to wait. We build more computers to hold more information, to produce more copies that ever, but we communicate less and less.

These are the times of fast foods and slow digestion, big men and small character, steep profits and shallow relationships. These are the days of two incomes, but more divorce, fancier houses, but broken homes. These are days of quick trips, disposable diapers, throwaway morality, one night stands, overweight bodies, and pills that do everything from cheer, to quiet, to kill. It is a time when there is much in the showroom window and nothing in the stockroom. A time when technology can bring this letter to you, and a time when you can choose either to share this insight, or to just hit delete.

Remember; spend some time with your loved ones, because they are not going to be around forever.

Remember, say a kind word to someone who looks up to you in awe, because that little person soon will grow up and leave your side.

Remember, to give a warm hug to the one next to you, because that is the only treasure you can give with your heart and it doesn't cost a cent.

Remember, to say, 'I Love You' to your partner and your loved ones, but most of all mean it. A kiss and an embrace will mend hurt when it comes from deep inside of you.

Remember to hold hands and cherish the moment for someday that person will no be there again.

Give time to love, give time to speak! And give time to share the precious thoughts in your mind.

AND ALWAYS REMEMBER: Life is not measured by the number of breaths we take, but by the moments that take our breath away.

—George Carlin

THOUGHTS FOR TODAY

A good friend will come and bail you out of jail, but a true friend will be sitting next to you saying, "Damn…that was fun".

You have always been so special in all the things you've said and done. I am so proud of you simply because you are my son (daughter).

My Daughter. All dreams I prayed you'd be are all the things you are – you were once my little girl – and now my shinning star.

When I was born, I was so surprised I didn't talk for a year and a half.

—Gracie Allen

CHOOSING FRIENDS

Choose your friends by their character and your socks by their color. Choosing your socks by their character makes no sense, and choosing your friends by their color is unthinkable.

—Anon

THE KISS

The only thing worth stealing is a kiss from a sleeping child.

—Joe Houldsworth

BE YOURSELF

There's no point in being grown up if you can't be childish sometimes.

—Doctor Who

EXCELLENCE VS PERFECTION

I am careful not to confuse excellence with perfection. Excellence I can reach for, perfection is God's Business.

—Michael J. Fox

BEING YOURSELF

When you are content to be simply yourself and don't compare or compete, everybody will respect you.

—Lao-Tzu

LAUGH

You don't stop laughing because you grow old. You grow old because you stop laughing.

—Michael Pritchard

INSTRUCTIONS FOR LIFE

- Take into account that great love and great achievements involve great risk.

- When you lose, don't lose the lesson.

- Follow the three R's

- Respect for self.

- Respect for other's and

- Responsibility for all your actions.

- Remember that not getting what you want is sometimes a wonderful stroke of luck.

- Learn the rules so you know who to break them properly.

- Don't let a little dispute injure a great relationship.

- When you realize you've made a mistake, take immediate steps to correct it.

- Spend some time alone every day.

- Open arms to change, but don't let go you your values.

- Remember that silence is sometimes the best answer.

- Life a good honorable life. Then when you get older and think back, you'll be able to enjoy it a second time.

- A loving atmosphere in your home is the foundation for your life.

- In disagreements with loved ones, deal only with the current situation. Don't bring up the past.

- Share your knowledge. It's a way to achieve immortality.

- Be gentle with the earth.

- Once a year, go someplace you've never been before.

- Remember that the best relationship is one in which your love for each other exceeds your need for each other.

- Judge your success by what you had to give up in order to get it.

- Approach love and cooking with reckless abandon.

You don't stop laughing when you get old, you get old when you stop laughing!

AS I'VE MATURED

I've learned that you cannot make someone love you. All you can do is stalk them and hope they panic and give in.

I've learned that one good turn gets most of the blanket.

I've learned that it takes years to build up trust, and it only takes suspicion, not proof, to destroy it.

I've learned that whatever hits the fan will not be evenly distributed.

I've learned that you shouldn't compare yourself to others – they are more screwed up than you think.

I've learned that depression is merely anger without enthusiasm.

I've learned that it is not what you wear; it is how you take it off.

I've learned that you can keep vomiting long after you think you're finished.

I've learned to not sweat the petty things, and not pet the sweat things.

I've learned that ex's are like fungus, and keep coming back.

I've learned age is a very high price to pay for maturity.

I've learned that I don't suffer from insanity, I enjoy it.

I've learned that we are responsible for what we do, unless we are celebrities.

I've learned that artificial intelligence is no match for natural stupidity.

I've learned that 99% of the time when something isn't working in your house, one of your kids did it.

I've learned that there is a fine line between genius and insanity.

I've learned that the people you care most about in life are taken from you too soon and all the less important ones just never go away. And the real pains in the ass are permanent.

If you don't have time to do something right, when will you find time to do it over?

One who lacks courage to start has already finished.

Make it a habit to do nice things for people who will never find out.

The best job for an employee who says, "Because that's the way we've always done it" is with the competition.

When complimented, a sincere 'thank you" is the only response required. Nothing else.

RULES TO LIVE BY

1. Never, under any circumstances, take a sleeping pill and a laxative on the same night.

2. Don't worry about what people think, they don't do it very often.

3. Going to church doesn't make you a Christian anymore than standing in a garage makes you a car.

4. Artificial intelligence is no match for natural stupidity.

5. If you must choose between two evils, pick the one you're never tried before.

6. My idea of housework is to sweep the room with a glance.

7. Not one shred of evidence supports the notion that life is serious.

8. A person, who is nice to you, but rude to the waiter, is not a nice person.

9. For every action, there is an equal and opposite government program.

10. If you look like your passport picture, you probably need the trip.

11. Bills travel through the mail at twice the speed of checks.

12. A conscience is what hurts when all of you other parts feel so good.

13. Eat well, stay fit, die anyway.

14. Men are from earth. Women are from earth. Deal with it.

15. No man has ever been shot while doing the dishes.

ALL I REALLY NEED TO KNOW, I LEARNED IN FOOTBALL

All I really need to know about how to live and what to do, I learned in football. You won't find wisdom at the top of a graduate school mountain but instead out on the practice field or on the game field.

- Share the pain and the triumphs.

- Leave the program better than when you entered.

- Give your teammates the credit due them when you are praised for accomplishments.

- Care about the well being of your opponent as well as respect them.

- Hard work and sweat is good for you.

- Live a balanced life – learn all you can, think before you do or say, enjoy the journey as well as the destination, have fun, get better every day, and take a break every now and then.

- When you meet a superior opponent, hold hands with you teammates and work together – that's the only way you can win.

- Believe in your teammates – If you try to do their job your fob will suffer.

- Maximum achievements are based on the hard work you put in before the season starts.

- Remember, the coach always wants what's best for the team – he isn't out to hurt anyone.

- Football is a game. Everyone loses – not only you. Defeat isn't fatal or final unless you allow it to be.

- The first and most important thing to learn is ATTITUDE!

- There is always a way to get your assignment done, even if your "problem" is bigger, faster, or stronger than you are.

- It's okay to pray. Aloud. In public. God doesn't care who wins the game. He cares about us. Our character. Our effort. The way we treat others.

- Tough times don't last – tough people do.

- To achieve something you've never had you have to DO SOMETHING you've never done.

- It is amazing what you can accomplish when no one cares who gets the credit.

- The desire to succeed is useless without the desire to prepare.

- Take anyone of life's problems and apply them to these principles whether your job, your nation – and they will still hold true.

- Think about what a better world it would be if we all got together to practice these qualities in late afternoons each day and then applied them on Friday nights as well as the rest of the week.

- We all live in a world that needs hard work, teamwork, sacrifice, unselfishness, and trust in your teammates.

- And remember, no matter how old you are, it will be your ATTITUDE and not the number of wins and loses that determine the quality of your life.

- Finally life becomes so simple if we can remember three simple rules:

- Do what you are supposed to do.

- Be where you are supposed to be.

- Say what you are supposed to say.

- Man's finest hour is that moment he has worked his heart out in a good cause and lies exhausted on the field of battle – VICTORIOUS!

- Learn to Listen. Next learn to formulate your thoughts. Then learn to argue effectively.

- Commitment, not authority creates results.

- Egotism is the anesthetic that dulls the pain of stupidity.

- I don't care if you lick windows,

- Take the special bus or occasionally pee on yourself.

- You hang in there sunshine, you're special.

- Every sixty seconds you spend angry, upset or mad, is a full minute of happiness you'll never get back.

- Today's Message:
  Life is short, break the rules.
  Forgive quickly.
  Kiss slowly.
  Love truly.
  Laugh uncontrollably.
  And never regret anything that made you smile.

- May your troubles be less, may your blessings be more, and

- May nothing but happiness come through your door.

- Don't take life so seriously! DANCE

THE LOMBARDI CREED

I owe most everything to football. A game which demands from each person a contribution of spirit! This spirit is the cohesive force that really binds eleven hardened, talented people into winners. The many (physical) hurts seem a small price to pay for having won, and there is no reason at all that is adequate for having lost!

To the winner is 100% elation, 100% laughter, 100% fun … and to the loser the only thing left is 100% resolution, and 100% determination!

Football is a game, I think, a great deal like life, in that a personal commitment be made toward success…toward victory…ultimate victory, which must be pursued with all of one's might!

Each week there is a new encounter…each year a new challenge… the color and display linger only in memory. But the spirit…the will to win…and the will to excel – these are the things that endure! These are the qualities which are so much more important that any of the events which occasion them!

The quality of any person's life has got to be a full measure of that person's own commitment to excellence ... and to victory regardless what field they may be in.

I would say that this is my creed for life.

My treasures do not clink, glitter or hang on the wall – they snuggle in the morning and say, "I love you daddy" at night.

EXECUTE WITH EXCELLENCE

- We will execute with excellence and will not compromise on the stringent security standards we provide to protect customer transactions and accounts.

- We will deliver the products and services that our customers want at fair prices.

- We will not compromise our high standards of customer service, safety and dependability.

LOVE YOU

Think about this for a minute…

If you happened to show up on my door step crying, I would care!

If you called me and asked me to pick you up because something happened, I would come!
If you had one day left to live your life, I would want to be a part of that last day!

If you needed a shoulder to cry on, I would give you mine!

This is a test to see who your real friends are or if you are just someone to talk to when they are bored.

Do you know what the relationship is between your two eyes?

They blink together, they move together, they cry together, they see things together, and they sleep together, but they never see each other; … that's what friendship is.

Life isn't about how you survived the storm…It's about how you dance in the rain!

SUPER BOWL

A man had 50 yard line tickets for the Super Bowl

As he sat down, he noticed that the seat next to him was empty.

He asked the man on the other side of the empty seat whether anyone was sitting there.

"No," the man replied, "The seat is empty."

"This is incredible," said the first man.

"Who in their right mind would have a seat like this for the Super Bowl, the biggest sporting event in the world and not use it?"

The second man replied, "Well, actually, the seat belongs to me. I was supposed to come with my wife, but she passed away. This will be the first Super Bowl we haven't been together since we got married in 1967."

"Oh, I'm sorry to hear that. That's terrible. But couldn't you find someone else—a friend or relative, or even a neighbor to take the seat?"

The man shook his head and said, "No, they're all at the funeral".

RANDOM THOUGHT

I've learned that pleasing everyone is impossible, but pissing everyone off is a piece of cake!

WISDOM

An old Cherokee told his grandson, "My son, there is a battle between two wolves inside us all. One is Evil. It is anger, jealousy, greed, resentment, inferiority, lies, and Ego. The other is Good. It is joy, peace, love, hope, humility, kindness, empathy, and truth."

The boy thought about it and asked, "Grandfather, which wolf wins?"

The old man quietly replied, "The one you feed."

Compiler's Bio

Robert D. Kramer is a graduate of Ohio University and served in the US Air Force during the Vietnam era. He has worked in the corporate America banking for forty-two years. Robert is also Director Emeritus for the Salvador Dali Museum in St. Petersburg, Florida and past Director of the Mahaffee Theater, also located in St. Petersburg, FL.

www.ingramcontent.com/pod-product-compliance
Lightning Source LLC
Chambersburg PA
CBHW071950040426
42447CB00009B/1300